Jack Altman

GW00937917

J·P·M

PUBLICATIONS

Victoria 39, South Coast 40, The Interior 42,
Pacific Rim National Park 44, Inside Passage 45,
Gulf Islands 45

Inland   **47**
Fraser and Thompson Canyons 47, Okanagan Valley 50

Rocky Mountains   **53**
British Columbia Rockies   **53**
Mount Revelstoke NP 53, Glacier NP 55,
Yoho NP 55, Kootenay NP 57
Alberta Rockies   **59**
Banff NP 59, Icefields Parkway 63, Jasper NP 65

Alberta and the Prairie Provinces   **69**
Calgary   **69**
Downtown 70, Fort Calgary 73,
Prince's Island 73, Calgary Stampede 74,
Head-Smashed-In Buffalo Jump 75

The Badlands   **77**
Drumheller 77, Edmonton 78

Prairie Capitals   **81**
Regina 82, Winnipeg 83

Nature Notes   **85**
Shopping 87, Dining Out 89, Sports 90
The Hard Facts   **92**
Index   96
Seattle, Washington USA   **97**

This Way Western Canada

Canada's West opens up to the visitor a great panoply of the country's fabled natural beauties. The vast region stretching beyond Ontario embraces endless prairies and the barren landscapes of the Badlands, rugged crags and tranquil lakes up in the Rocky Mountains, orchards and vineyards in the sunny Okanagan Valley, and mighty rivers flowing through deep canyons and past lofty pine forests to the Pacific Ocean. Apart from in the higher altitudes of the Rockies, the climate is blessedly milder than any of the preconceived images you might have of Canadian weather. In British Columbia's southwest corner around Vancouver, it is positively mellow, refreshed by the occasional shower of rain.

The area generally known as Western Canada comprises over two-thirds of the country's total land surface. Canada as a whole, covering more than 9,970,000 sq km (around 3,850,000 sq miles), is bigger than the neighbouring United States and second in the world only to Russia. Geographically, the western region includes the Yukon and Northwest Territories, but this Far North is usually off the tourists' beaten track.

Slightly tamer sides of the wilderness are to be found in the splendid opportunities for outdoor sports: fishing—salmon and trout in the rivers and myriad lakes, sea bass and more salmon in the Pacific—sailing, canoeing, whitewater-rafting, camping, hiking, climbing. From early winter to late spring, there's magnificent skiing at BC's Whistler or in the Rockies, where Calgary staged the 1988 Olympics. And families can enjoy the genteel pleasures of swimming or windsurfing along the fine sandy beaches of Vancouver Island.

BC's forests represent only 17 per cent of the country's total but provide more than half of its timber and most of its other wood products, too. In the great conifer woods thriving in the mild damp climate along the Pacific coast and on Vancouver Island, the kings are the great Douglas firs, towering above the cedar, balsam fir, hemlock and Sitka spruce.

Alberta's wealth has come from some of the world's richest oilfields. But the province's landscape is more appreciated for the splendid snowcapped Rockies that rise above sprawling prairies where Indians once hunted buffalo and where now superb beef

cattle graze. The awesome Badlands east of Calgary were, over a hundred million years ago, the stomping grounds of dinosaurs, and their bones are still being dug up and displayed in the great museum at Drumheller.

The Towns and the People

The region is not just one big wilderness. The vast majority of the population is concentrated down on the southern strip along the US border. On the Pacific coast, Vancouver is one of the world's most civilized cities. The moderate climate makes living nice and easy in an idyllic setting of ocean, river and pine-forested mountains—which still dwarf the downtown skyscrapers. Its strategic position commanding commerce with all the powers of the Pacific Rim has made Vancouver's port the busiest and most prosperous of Canada. It has attracted immigrants not just from Britain but from all over Europe and Asia.

Over on Vancouver Island, Victoria, the provincial capital, demonstrates in its unabashed quaintness just how really, almost unreally, British British Columbia can be—with a genteel citizenry to match.

Contemplating the work of nature at Moraine Lake.

In Alberta, against the spectacular backdrop of the Rockies, the gleaming skyscraper city of Calgary bears all the bold, even brazen marks of its petroleum boom years in the 1970s and 80s. Often more Texan than Canadian, like Houston or Dallas, it has transformed its cattlemen into oilmen and bankers. But in July, the famous Calgary Stampede of rodeo, wagon races and other cowboy shenanigans still reigns supreme.

If Calgary handles the transportation and financing of Alberta's oil and natural gas, Edmonton, the provincial capital to the north, is the production centre. In a province not otherwise renowned for its cultural activity, Edmonton stages several first-class arts festivals. But its most extraordinary monument is what has gone down in the *Guinness Book of World Records* as the world's largest shopping centre, the West Edmonton Mall.

And there are also the first people of Western Canada, now known as exactly that: the First People—the American Indians of BC and Alberta and, in the Northwest Territories, the Inuit. After more than a century of decline and neglect, the people who first settled the country are now reaffirming their identity and culture, and reclaiming their lands and economic rights.

5

Baffin Bay

GREENLAND

Baffin Island

Auyuittuq National Park

Prince Charles Island

Foxe

Basin

Southampton Island

Cape Dorset

Lake Harbour

Labrador Sea

ATLANTIC OCEAN

Salluit

Ungava Bay

Aupaluk

Povungnituk

Kuujjuaq

Inukjuak

LABRADOR

North West River

Goose Bay

Battle Harbour

Saint Anthony

Hudson Bay

Schefferville

NEWFOUNDLAND

Caniapiscau

Esker

Labrador City

Gander

Saint John's

NEWFOUNDLAND

Belcher Islands

Havre-Saint-Pierre

Corner Brook

Grand Bay

Winisk Wild River Prov. Park

Chisasibi

QUÉBEC

Sept-Îles

Channel-Port-aux-Basques

James Bay

Akimiski Island

Némiscau

Baie-Comeau

Gaspé

Gulf of St. Lawrence

ONTARIO

Moosonee

Chibougamau

Jonquière

Rimouski

PRINCE EDWARD ISLAND

Charlottetown

Sydney

Central Patricia

Haute Maurice Prov. Park

Chicoutimi

NEW BRUNSWICK

Moncton

Armstrong

Nakina

Rouyn

Val-d'Or

Laurentides Prov. Park

Québec

Trois-Rivières

Saint John

Halifax

NOVA SCOTIA

Nipigon

Timmins

La Vérendrye Prov. Park

Montréal

Thunder Bay

Sault Ste-Marie

North Bay

Ottawa

Lake Superior

Sudbury

Boston

ATLANTIC OCEAN

Duluth

Lake Huron

Toronto

Lake Ontario

Minneapolis

Hamilton

Lake Michigan

London

Niagara Falls

New York

CANADA

Detroit

Windsor

Cleveland

Chicago

Lake Erie

Saint-Laurent

WEST CANADA

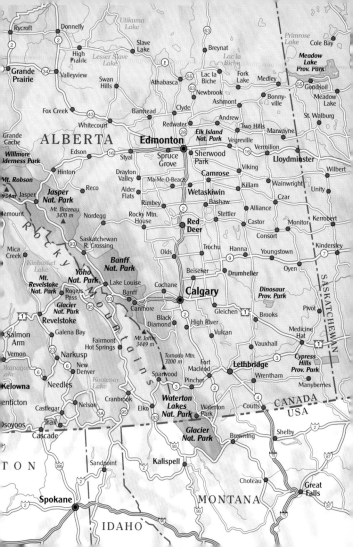

Flashback

Beginnings

The melting of the ice has always played a vital role in Canadian life. For hunting or fishing, farming or gardening, the thaw signals a time of movement and renewal. Naturally enough, then, the human history of Canada's western regions begins with the end of the last Ice Age, at most 25,000 years, but more like 10–12,000 years ago. The snow and ice receded to reveal what the scientists call Beringia, more than a land bridge, a vast land mass (now submerged) linking Asia and North America. From the fossilized remains of mammoth, bison, caribou and musk-oxen, and the stone weapons used to hunt them, it has been surmised that several waves of hunters from Siberia pursued their prey to Alaska and later south into Canada. Scientists suggest that the first people to have reached the western regions left traces carbon-dated some 9,000 years old, notably at Charlie Lake Cave in the northeast corner of British Columbia.

Hats off in style for Canada Day, celebrated on 1st July.

The migrants followed two main routes: the first into British Columbia along the Pacific coast, where they settled into villages to live off the abundant shellfish, salmon and whales; and others east of the Rockies into Alberta, where they led a more nomadic life of hunters.

The Europeans Arrive

Our knowledge of human development in the west before the modern era still remains sketchy. Archaeological evidence shows that by at least 500 BC, Salish Indians had settled in the area of Vancouver and Vancouver Island. Others, circling north from the Mississippi Valley, were cultivating fruit and vegetables in the southern prairies of Alberta and Saskatchewan around AD 200.

The pivotal moment in Canadian history is known momentously as "Contact", the Indians' encounter with European civilization. Scholars characterize the country's artistic, religious, social and economic life as pre- or post-Contact. The Indians' first confrontation with the newcomers' culture was not with people but with their horses. Introduced in the southern plains from Mexico by the Spanish *conquistadores* in

11

CANADA, OH CANADA

Scholars claim the country's name comes from 16th-century French explorer Jacques Cartier hearing an Iroquois Indian word, *kanata*, meaning town or group of dwellings. Another explanation suggests early Spanish explorers returned from a fruitless quest for gold and declared: "*Aca nada*"—"There is nothing here."

the 16th century, the horses reached Canada, through inter-tribal trade and raiding, by the 1730s. At first the animals just made it possible to transport heavier materials for bigger and better dwellings, but they soon radically transformed the Plains Indians' hunting and warfare techniques. They were no longer obliged to stalk buffalo herds on foot to drive them over cliffs. And horse raiding itself became a socially prestigious, by no means shameful pursuit.

Further dramatic changes followed the arrival out west of the first French and British fur traders, armed with guns, even though at first the buffalo-hunters preferred their bows and arrows, which hit their targets more accurately. The French also brought good cognac and the British bad gin—which they attempted to pass as brandy by colouring it

with iodine. Neither tipple boded well for the Indians' well-being.

At the same time, European navigators began appearing on the Pacific coast. In 1774, the Spaniard Juan Pérez Hernández became the first European to chart the northerly Queen Charlotte Islands along the coast of British Columbia. At stake, in competition with Russian ships sailing south from Siberia, was the valuable trade in sea otter pelts with the Nootka Indians. Bad weather stopped Hernández from landing and claiming the territory for Spain.

Four years later, two British ships under Captain James Cook put into Nootka Sound on Vancouver Island. Cook had sailed eastwards across the Pacific in search of the coveted northwest passage around North America. He repaired his ships, traded for otter pelts with the prosperous Nootka hunters and fishermen and sailed away a month later.

In 1789, the Spanish returned to assert their exclusive rights to a trading post at Nootka Sound and to dispute Britain's claim to the BC coast. Three years later, under a British threat of war and without support from its traditional French ally—which was busy at the time with the Revolution—Spain was forced to share trading rights and later withdrew completely.

At home in the Rockies, the redoubtable black bear.

Opening Up the West

After the British victory in Quebec in 1759, the French army abandoned "New France", leaving exploitation of the lands west of Ontario to rival fur traders of the rather staid conservative Hudson's Bay Company (HBC), and later to the more adventurous North West Company, formed in 1783 and based in Montreal. The Nor'westers' intrepid explorer Alexander Mackenzie was the first European to travel overland to Canada's Pacific coast. In 1793, he set out from the company's trading post at Fort Chipepwan on Lake Athabasca in northeast Alberta. Using Indian scouts to cross the Rocky Mountains, he canoed along the Peace and Upper Fraser rivers, finally leaving the waterways to strike out across the Chilcotin Plateau and Coast Mountains to the Bella Coola Inlet leading to the Queen Charlotte Islands.

Some 15 years later, Simon Fraser and David Thompson established fur trading posts that developed into BC's first European settlements—New Caledonia, Fort Macleod, Fort Fraser and Prince George. Fraser, the North West Company's director of operations west of the Rockies, was the son of a British Loyalist who had moved to Canada from 13

Vermont during the American War of Independence. He explored what was to become the Fraser River through its mighty canyon all the way to the ocean. His fellow Nor'wester Thompson, a London-born geographer who had earlier mapped the Athabasca and Saskatchewan rivers, was busy following the Columbia River from its source all the way into Oregon to its mouth on the Pacific. Thompson arrived a couple of weeks after

LEAVING A GOOD NAME

The man who negotiated the Anglo-Spanish agreement on coastal trading rights in 1792 was Captain George Vancouver. Born in King's Lynn, England, the 35-year-old navigator had served under Cook in the South Seas and on the first British expedition along the northwest coast. The conflict with Spain interrupted a three-year mapping voyage from Oregon to Alaska, naming bays, inlets and coastal landmarks as he went. After recovering British properties seized by the Spanish, he returned to an early retirement in London, where he died in 1798. A century later, the modest sailor's name was perpetuated when given to BC's best-known city and island.

American explorers—who had travelled overland and were building Fort Astoria to stake the US claim to the Oregon territory. (The Oregon Treaty, signed by Britain and the US in 1846, fixed BC's southern border at the 49th parallel except for Vancouver Island, where the Hudson's Bay Company had set up its western headquarters at Fort Victoria three years before.)

Amalgamated with the North West Company since 1821, HBC had constructed in the west an empire which was too lucrative for the British and colonial Canadian governments to leave it in private hands any longer. Gold was discovered first in the Queen Charlotte Islands, then along the Fraser River and later in the remote Cariboo Mountains, each time attracting thousands of prospectors from California. The British put an end to the HBC's trading privileges in 1858, buying off its hot-tempered boss, Sir James Douglas, with the governorship of the newly created British Columbia, a name chosen by Queen Victoria in preference to New Caledonia, New Cornwall, New Hanover or New Georgia. After a brief spell in New Westminster, the province's capital was set up in Douglas's hometown of Victoria when Vancouver Island was united to the mainland in 1867.

On Track For Nationhood

That same year, 1867, the British North America Act created the Dominion of Canada, but BC's 12,000 white residents did not vote to join the confederation until 1871, when the federal government agreed to build a transcontinental railway, the future Canadian Pacific (CPR), linking the province to the eastern markets. Completion was promised within ten years and the subsequent delay nearly prompted BC to secede.

Meanwhile, east of the Rockies, British surveyors reported potentially excellent farmland in the Saskatchewan, Assiniboine and Red river valleys—contrary to the HBC's attempts to downplay the viability of the Prairies. In 1870, the Canadian government took over the rest of HBC's western territory which later became the provinces of Saskatchewan, Manitoba and Alberta.

Railway construction began in Ontario in 1875 and five years later from the other direction at Yale, BC. A workforce of 13,500 hacked an eastward path through Kicking Horse Pass in the Rockies to the plains. Over 9,000 of the workers were Chinese, contracted from California at half-pay and habitually saddled with the most hazardous, often fatal tasks high on sheer rock walls above plunging canyons. Many had previously worked as miners in the Cariboo Mountains during the 1860s gold rush.

In 1885, the railway's completion ran up against the ongoing armed struggle for the Manitoba land rights of Métis descendants of Indians and French fur traders. Led by the fiery Louis Riel, the fight, which at first enjoyed the support of Anglo-Saxon farmers, was also for cultural equality of French and English schools and

KINGS OF THE PLAINS

The best known of the Plains Indians are the Blackfoot who, through Hollywood Westerns and Buffalo Bill rodeo shows, present the stock image of feathered headdress, buckskin costume, warpaint and the Sundance performed prior to the buffalo hunt. At the height of their power, they covered much of modern Alberta and Montana and still occupy lands from the North Saskatchewan River to the Missouri River. They are in fact three tribes allied in language and warfare: the Blackfoot proper (*Siksika* meaning "black feet" from having walked across burnt prairie grass); the Bloods or *Kainai* meaning "many chiefs"; and the Peigan or *Pikuni*, from their legendary "scabby robes" made from improperly prepared hides.

15

Vibrant, sophisticated, Vancouver twinkles on the brink of the Pacific Ocean.

churches. After the death of an *agent provocateur* from Toronto, Ontario troops were sent in—by train— and the rebellion was crushed. The transcontinental railway was finally completed in November 1885, with the famous "Last Spike" being driven into the track at Craigellachie, BC. The first passenger train to cross Canada left Montreal on June 28, 1886, and arrived at Port Moody in Vancouver on July 4.

Despite the expropriated lands and the toll in human life, as well as mass extermination of buffalo herds impeding the railway's progress, this great engineering feat was of enormous symbolic importance to national unity. The railway transformed the sleepy trading post of Winnipeg and the log fort at Calgary into cities, while the Pacific terminus turned the little township of Granville into the great port-city of Vancouver. The CPR's own hotels opened up the tourist industry, from Quebec City's Château Frontenac to Banff Springs Hotel and Château Lake Louise in the Rockies and Victoria's Empress Hotel on Vancouver Island.

The 20th Century
From 1896 to World War I, the population of the Prairie Provinces was boosted by intensive

16

immigration. Manitoba attracted large numbers of Eastern Europeans, above all Ukrainians who today constitute 11 per cent of the its population. Wheat exports soared in World War I. Farmers poured into Alberta from eastern Canada, the US and Britain. Edmonton boomed as the supply centre for the 1898 Klondike gold rush up in the Yukon.

Alberta's provincehood was achieved in 1905 amid bitter conflicts with the federal government over rights to exploit natural resources, the Catholic minority's right to public-funded schools and the choice of Edmonton over Calgary as capital. The disputes created Alberta's enduring hostility to federal involvement in local affairs, particularly after the 1931 Statute of Westminster gave Canada full autonomy in home and foreign affairs. Alberta's governments have remained staunchly conservative.

With rotting wheat surpluses followed by ten years of bad harvests and drought, the Depression years were known in the Prairie Provinces as the Dirty Thirties. BC's lumber industry slumped after years of high profits.

Saskatchewan distinguished itself in 1944 by electing North America's first socialist government—the Cooperative Commonwealth Federation. But the first national prime minister to come from Saskatchewan, John Diefenbaker, was a Conservative (1957–62), whose big wheat deal with China tripled their incomes.

Alberta's great leap forward came from oil, discovered in 1914 in Turney Valley south of Calgary and exploited in earnest after the great Leduc oilfield strike in 1947. This paid off after the 1973 international oil-pricing crisis. BC benefited from the opening up of Asian markets on the Pacific Rim. Vancouver captured worldwide attention with its enormously successful Expo 86. This emphasized transportation and communications and expanded perception of the BC economy beyond the traditional image of forestry. Similarly, the 1988 Winter Olympics put Calgary's name on the map as an attractive tourist destination for access to the Canadian Rockies. The positive image of western Canada has been highlighted in the 1990s by its being first choice for the more prosperous émigrés from Hong Kong—in addition to the fairweather seekers from Ontario, Quebec and the Maritime provinces. In the 1997 federal elections, BC, Alberta and Saskatchewan all swung from the Liberals to the right-wing Reform party. In the face of federal encroachments, the west seemed more determined than ever to hold on to its prosperity.

British Columbia

The magnetism of Canada's beautiful province on the Pacific remains the constant call of its grand outdoors. Look up from the skyscraper canyons of downtown Vancouver and you will see to the north the beckoning snowcapped peaks and wooded slopes of the Coast Mountains that dominate a shoreline deeply indented with fjords.

Answer the call and visit the summer and winter mountain resort of Whistler along the old Squamish road, now spruced up and renamed the Sea to Sky Highway.

VANCOUVER
Downtown, Chinatown, Stanley Park, Granville Island, English Bay, North Shore, Sea to Sky Highway

Often to the chagrin—and perhaps not a little envy—of Canadians "back east", this town has more affinities with its American neighbours south along the Pacific coast than with fellow Canadian cities on the other side of the Rockies. Vancouver seems to share a taste for good living with San Francisco and its renowned relaxed atmosphere with Los Angeles, but also a real, if cleverly camouflaged dynamism with Seattle.

The quality of life here is due in no small part to its ethnic diversification. In addition to migrants from Canada's cooler eastern provinces, the descendants of the town's British, predominantly Scottish founding fathers have been joined by a cosmopolitan mix of Germans, Jews, Italians, Eastern Europeans, Chinese, in increasing numbers from Hong Kong and Taiwan, Japanese who have long found the city's temperate climate familiar and congenial, and Sikhs from the Indian and Pakistani Punjab.

The city is surrounded on three sides by water—English Bay and Burrard Inlet to the north, Georgia Strait to the west and Fraser River to the south. So get to know the bridges that link the centre to

Totem poles of the Northwest Coast Indians in Stanley Park.

MUNICIPALITY OF NORTH VANCOUVER

MUNICIPALITY OF BURNABY

Burrard Inlet

Lynn Park

Keith Rd.

Keith St.

Confederation Park

Hastings St.

Lougheed Highway

Grandview Hy.

Kingsway

Central Park

Boundary Rd.

Central Park

Drive

Mahon Park

13th St.

City Hall

Exhibition Park

Rd.

Renfrew

22nd Ave.

27th Ave.

45th Ave.

54th Ave.

Fraser View Golf Course

S.E. Marine

Nanaimo St.

Drive

Clark Drive

Victoria

Grandview Hwy.

Kingsway

Victoria Drive

Victoria Drive

S.E. Marine Drive

Fraser River

North Arm

Fraser St.

Fraser

Hastings St.

Lumberman's Arch

Aquarium

Coal Harbour

Canada Place

Expo Centre

Georgia St.

Auditorium

False Creek

City Hall

Queen Elizabeth Park

King Edward Ave.

33rd Ave.

41st

Langara Golf Club

Main St.

Lions Gate Bridge

Stanley Park

Lost Lagoon

DOWNTOWN

Maritime Museum

Kitsilano Beach

Arbutus St.

Kerrisdale Arena

Oak St.

Granville St.

10th St.

Ave.

Ave.

Ave.

41st Ave.

Dunbar St.

Golf Course

Grauer Rd.

Ferguson Rd.

English Bay

Spanish Banks Beach

Jericho Beach

4th St.

10th Ave.

16th Ave.

33rd Ave.

Alma St.

Golf Course

S.W. Marine Drive

S.W. Marine Drive

Musqueam Indian Reserve

Iona Island

Sea Island

Strait of Georgia

University of British Columbia

Pt. Grey

N

0 1 2 3 km
0 1 2 miles

VANCOUVER

its outskirts. False Creek, cutting into the city from English Bay, is spanned by three traffic bridges joining the downtown and West End area to the rest of Vancouver: from east to west, Cambie, Granville and Burrard. The main bridge across Burrard Inlet is Lion's Gate, leading to the North Shore neighbourhoods of North and West Vancouver, the ferry harbour at Horseshoe Bay and the Sea to Sky Highway up to Whistler. (Eastern Vancouver is linked to the North Shore by the 2nd Narrows Bridge.)

Take advantage of the first-rate bus system, especially as a cheap and easy way of making your first sightseeing tours. The number 1 bus starts out from old Gastown through the centre to English Bay Beach and back; from the centre's West End, the 52 loops around Stanley Park; and the 250 takes you from Georgia Street over to the North Shore via West Vancouver to Horseshoe Bay.

Downtown

The business, shopping and entertainment centre stands on the West End peninsula separating English Bay from the Burrard Inlet. For a city little over a century old, there are no grand historic monuments, but plenty of fine modern architecture to express Vancouver's present-day prosperity.

Robson Street

Start out from this perfect people-watching place, the pulse of downtown Vancouver. There is plenty of action day and night

---

VANCOUVER HIGHLIGHTS

– **Capilano River Park**: cable car up Grouse Mountain and spectacular suspension bridge over deep canyon (p. 31).
– **Chinatown**: keeping alive traditions of Chinese community with market, restaurants and craft shops (p. 27).
– **Gastown**: historic neighbourhood of old warehouses turned into shops and cafés (p. 25).
– **Granville Island**: lively public market, waterfront cafés, theatres and galleries (p. 29).
– **Museum of Anthropology**: Northwest Coast Indian art in magnificent modern clifftop building (p. 29).
– **Stanley Park**: take the Sea Wall promenade around forest wilderness and beaches (p. 27).

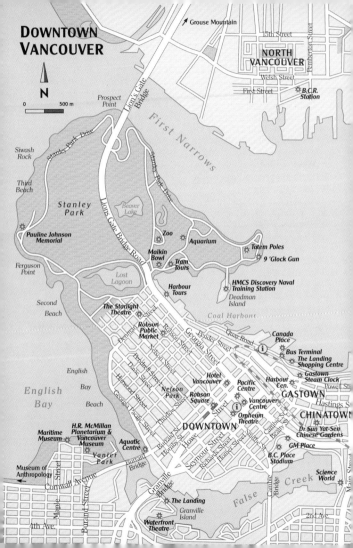

DOWNTOWN VANCOUVER

N

0   500 m

→ Grouse Mountain

15th Street

NORTH VANCOUVER

Welsh Street

First Street

⭐ B.C.R. Station

Lion's Gate Bridge

Prospect Point

First Narrows

Stanley Park Drive

Siwash Rock

Third Beach

Stanley Park

Beaver Lake

Lions Gate Bridge Road

⭐ Pauline Johnson Memorial

⭐ Zoo

⭐ Aquarium

⭐ Totem Poles

9 'Clock Gun

Ferguson Point

Malkin Bowl

Tram Tours

HMCS Discovery Naval Training Station

Deadman Island

Lost Lagoon

Harbour Tours

Coal Harbour

Second Beach

The Starlight Theatre

Quay Road

Canada Place

ℹ

Bus Terminal
The Landing
Shopping Centre

English Bay

Robson Public Market

Robson Street

Georgia Street

Pender Street

Hotel Vancouver

Pacific Centre

Harbour Cen.

⭐ Gastown Steam Clock

Powell St.

GASTOWN

Nelson Park

Robson Square

Vancouver Centre

Hastings S.

English Bay Beach

Nicola Street

Broughton Street

Jervis Street

Bute Street

Thurlow Street

ℹ

Orpheum Theatre

CHINATOWN

Georgia Pacific Street

DOWNTOWN

Street

Dr Sun Yat-Sen Chinese Gardens

H.R. McMillan Planetarium & Vancouver Museum

Maritime Museum

Aquatic Centre

Burrard Street

Seymour Street

Richards Street

Homer Street

Smithe St.

GM Place

B.C. Place Stadium

Vanier Park

Howe Street

Hornby St.

Science World

Museum of Anthropology

Cornwall Avenue

Burrard Bridge

Granville Bridge

False Creek

Cambie Bridge

Maple Street

4th Ave.

The Landing

Granville Island

Waterfront Theatre

2nd Ave.

Main Street

along the tree-lined street's cafés, restaurants, boutiques and department stores. The two blocks west of Burrard, once known as "Robsonstrasse" because of the German immigrants there, now offer a cosmopolitan mixture of Japanese, Italian, Scandinavian and Vietnamese restaurants.

Robson Square

On the street's 800 block, this imaginative piece of modern urban design sets hanging gardens and a reflector pool around a sunken plaza of shops and cafés where you can pause a while to contemplate the neighbouring skyscrapers. Among them is the venerable Hotel Vancouver, a 1970s work of the city's celebrated master builder, Arthur Erickson, and landscape architect Cornelia Oberlander.

Provincial Law Courts

Erickson's revolutionary structure at 800 Smithe aims to make usually forbidding law courts as publicly appealing as his nearby Robson Square. In place of the classical marble-columned "temple", the courthouse is an essentially horizontal edifice where people are invited to stroll around bright and airy walkways of glass, steel and concrete on seven tiers linked by a maze of ramps and stairways. Watered by cascading pools, gardens are every-

where, indoor and outdoor, with rose bushes, flowering shrubs, orange trees, even a miniature pine forest—after all, this is BC.

Vancouver Art Gallery

The municipal collection, mainly of Canadian artists, is housed in the province's original, more stately courthouse. This early 1900s neo-Palladian building is by Francis Rattenbury, designer of Victoria's Parliament Buildings and the Empress Hotel, and renovated by Erickson. Besides a few European paintings, the collection also includes American works by Andy Warhol and Roy Lichtenstein, but the principal artist featured here is Emily Carr (1871–1945). Her idiosyncratic painting treats the BC landscape with energetic flourishes that bring to the totemic themes of the Indians the dynamic technique of the French post-Impressionists with whom she studied. A natural eccentric, she used to wheel her pet monkey around the streets of Victoria. Regulars at her boarding house knew here as Crazy Old Millie, while to her friends among the Kwakiutl Indians she was the Laughing One.

Christ Church Cathedral

At the corner of Burrard and Georgia, this handsome 19th-century neo-Gothic edifice is Vancouver's oldest surviving church. 23

Take a look within at the fine stained-glass windows and the superb hammer-beam timber ceiling. The Anglican church only narrowly escaped the wrecker's ball in the 1970s building boom and received an "architectural apology" from the adjacent post-modern tower—built in 1990 with a neo-Gothic lobby and named Cathedral Place.

Granville Street

The main street for cinemas and theatres. The Orpheum (N° 884), once a movie house and now home of the Vancouver Symphony Orchestra, has an exotic Spanish Renaissance interior with mock-Gothic vaulting and Moorish arches. Look out, too, for the splendid if somewhat rundown Art Deco façade of the 1940s Vogue Theatre (N° 929).

Vancouver Central Public Library

Vaguely familiar? Yes, this gently curving, russet-coloured colossus (south of Homer between Robson and Georgia) is a striking—admirers say elegant—pastiche of Rome's Colosseum. It is the somewhat contested 1995 work of Israeli-born Canadian architect Moshe Safdie, designer of the controversial Habitat modular housing for Montreal's Expo 67 and Ottawa's National Gallery. Beyond the Georgia Street entrance, an airy circular promenade with boutiques, cafés and a bookshop links the seven-storey library to an adjacent federal office tower. The library proper is housed in a brightly lit rectangular core of free-access stacks with reading areas looking out onto the city.

VIEWS—FROM ABOVE AND BELOW

For an overall view of Vancouver's beautiful skyline, cross to the North Shore on Lion's Gate Bridge to the Capilano Road where a cable car takes you up Grouse Mountain for a spectacular panorama of city and harbour. Downtown, there is an observation deck at the top of the 40-storey Harbour Centre (555 West Hastings). For a bargain-price view from the harbour itself, cross Burrard Inlet on the public Seabus plying between its terminus, at the foot of Granville Street, and North Vancouver—12 minutes each way. A 90-minute Harbour Ferries cruise departs from Coal Harbour through Lion's Gate Bridge and around Stanley Park for a look at the busy commercial port, too. But some of the best views of the skyline with its mountain backdrop are the glimpses you catch between streets sloping down to the south shore of False Creek.

Like a huge ship at anchor, sails caught by the wind: Canada Place.

Yaletown

Three blocks southwest of the library, the Canadian Pacific Railway's old service yard and decaying warehouse district has been converted into a charming neighbourhood of restaurants, furniture shops, bars, offices and loft-style apartments. Bounded by Nelson, Granville and Pacific Boulevard, the once purely functional constructions of brick and wood post-and-beam are now the ultimate in chic for Vancouver's trendy architects, designers and media princes. Join them at their favourite watering-place, the Yaletown Brewing Co., *the* pub on Hamilton Street.

Canada Place

Originally the Canada Pavilion for Vancouver's Expo 86, this convention centre, hotel and cruise ship terminal heads out into the Burrard Inlet like the prow of a 19th-century sailing ship. The white "sails" forming its roof are made of Teflon-coated fibreglass. The city's main tourist information centre is almost directly opposite the pavilion, across the harbourfront highway at 200 Burrard.

Gastown

The historic neighbourhood's refurbished brick, wood and stone buildings along cobbled streets 25 extend east along Water Street from Richards to Carrall. Together, the outdoor cafés, restaurants and boutiques make an appealing conversion of the Victorian warehouses and dollar-a-night commercial hotels built here after the original Gastown burned down in 1886. The statue of founding father "Gassy Jack"

BRICKS, GAS AND STEEL

The city began life inauspiciously in 1862 when three failed British gold-prospectors failed again with a brickworks built just south of what is now Stanley Park. With all that timber around, nobody wanted bricks. Five years later, retired riverboat captain John Deighton opened a saloon for thirsty workers from the nearby Hastings lumber mill. The talkative saloon-keeper, "Gassy Jack", prospered and attracted a whole community to the area. It was known first as Gastown, then more soberly as Granville. When the CPR's tracks were laid there for its western terminus in 1886, Gastown went out with a flourish, by burning to the ground. The town was quickly rebuilt, this time using the bricks previously spurned, and a golden future opened up for what CPR's general manager insisted be renamed Vancouver.

Deighton stands on Maple Tree Square, starting-point for a free 90-minute guided walking tour (daily in summer, 2 p.m.). His saloon stood across the square at Byrnes Block (2 Water Street, originally the Alhambra Hotel), notable for the decorative Italian-style cornice along the roof. Nearby, the smithy, stables and butcher shops of Blood Alley Square have been transformed, along with the police station of Gaoler's Mews, into delightful tree-shaded courtyards in which to buy a quaint hat or dress or just sip a cappuccino or beer.

At the west end of Water Street, what is touted without contest as the world's first steam-powered clock blows a whistle on the hour. Nearby, Gaslight Square (N° 131) is an imaginative modern building housing the Architecture Institute of British Columbia. The Landing (N° 361) is a tastefully converted water-front warehouse.

Two Stadiums

Vancouver professional sports teams play at the east end of the downtown peninsula. The BC Lions football team try to crunch opponents under the huge dome of BC Place while the Huskies basketballers and Canucks ice-hockeymen share the smaller General Motors Place next door, locally nicknamed The Garage.

Chinatown

Stretching along Pender and Keefer streets east of Carrall, the historic neighbourhood of Vancouver's Chinese community, descendants of the Canadian Pacific's railway workers, has gone through considerable changes in recent years. Growing prosperity, together with the influx of affluent immigrants from Hong Kong, has drawn many of the original families out to the suburbs, particularly Richmond. But the neighbourhood's daytime bustle continues among its fishmongers and markets, shops selling silks, Chinese—and BC—jade, bamboo and lacquer ware, traditional medicines of herbs, spices and other ancient potions for aches, pains and impotence, as well as restaurants with alluring displays of barbecued pork and duck.

On the corner of Carrall and Pender, the Chinese Freemasons Building was erected in 1901 with a name intended to ward off racism, prevalent at the time. What is in fact a traditional fraternal community organization, with no link to Freemasonry whatsoever, has a conciliatory European façade on Carrall, reserving its Chinese-style recessed balconies for Pender.

Behind the Chinese Cultural Centre at 50 East Pender, devoted to Chinese arts and crafts, is the Dr Sun Yat-Sen Garden. Designed by artists from Suzhou, capital of classical Chinese garden landscaping, it proposes a microcosm of nature in which opposites are balanced according to the Taoist philosophy of yin and yang—rough stone and smooth water, shadow and light—and human qualities symbolized by different shrubs.

Stanley Park

It is difficult to imagine a finer setting than this headland commanding the eastern end of English Bay. No conventionally man-

---

STRICTLY CASUAL

To twist a phrase, you can get a Canadian out of the backwoods, but you can't get the backwoods out of the Canadian. The time-honoured image of people in BC still dressing like pioneers has been handed down by the lusty lumberjacks of whom "Johnny Canuck" was the legendary archetype. He remains the province's fashion model, even in increasingly sophisticated Vancouver. The city's ice hockey team, not wildly successful but nonetheless hugely popular, is known as the Canucks, and the slick business-suited front-office guys get down to basic baggy jeans and sturdy bright check shirts as soon as they leave the stadium.

icured city park, it did not need artificial landscaping to enhance the majestic stands of red cedar, maple, hemlock, Sitka spruce, lodgepole pine and Douglas fir, cleared only for beaches and a few picnic tables at the ocean's edge. The rainforest, still at its heart an almost impenetrable wilderness with trees perhaps over 800 years old, originally provided timber for Salish Indians' cabins and totem poles and then, as the First Narrows Military Reserve until 1886, shipmasts and spars for Britain's Royal Navy.

What is now one of the world's handsomest city parks takes its name from Canada's governor-general, Lord Stanley. His bronze statue stands north of the downtown park entrance at the foot of Georgia Street.

Sea Wall Promenade

You can hire a bicycle to tackle the splendid ocean-front walk, 10^1/$_2$ km (6^1/$_2$ miles) long. Head east past the Royal Vancouver Yacht Club and a causeway leading to Deadman's Island, the somewhat irreverent name for a Salish burial ground and now a last remnant of the naval training base.

At Hallelujah Point, where the Salvation Army held its revivalist meetings, is the Nine O'Clock Gun, electronically timed to fire at 9 p.m., originally signalling the fishing curfew. At Brockton Point, eastern edge of the park, the sea wall turns west past a group of 19th-century Haida and Kwakiutl totem poles brought from BC's north coast. Britain's cultural contribution can be witnessed on a nearby field, the scene of the bizarre ritual known as cricket. Out on the seaward side again is a bronze statue named *Girl in a Wet Suit*, a resolutely modern North American version of Copenhagen's famous mermaid.

Vancouver Aquarium

Accessible from the eastern arm of the Sea Wall or from Coal Harbour, this impressive collection of fish, sea mammals, birds and reptiles gives an excellent insight into the creatures of the Pacific, BC's inland lakes and rivers and the tropical fauna of the Amazonian rainforest. There are the usual dolphin shows, but also sharks, beluga and killer whales, nicer seals and sea otters and nasty tarantulas, poisonous frogs, giant cockroaches, boa constrictors, piranhas. Something for everyone.

The Beaches

The sandy beaches are along the park's western edge, well-equipped with restaurants, cafés, picnic tables and facilities for fishing, tennis, golf-putting and a swimming pool at Second Beach. Looking out to sea, Siwash Rock presents the petrified form of a legendary Salish Indian hero who purified himself in the waters of English Bay for his new-born child. Just east of the Pitch and Putt Golf course, Lost Lagoon is a lake of reclaimed marshland and tidal inlet popular with trumpeter swans, mallards, coots and Canada geese.

Granville Island

The heart of the island is a delightful public market surrounded by arts and crafts galleries, three theatres, shops, bars and good restaurants. Always linked to the mainland by the Granville Bridge causeways, the island was created from drained mud flats in False Creek back in 1915 as a factory area for sawmills, ironworks, chemicals and other heavy industry. All except a cement works have gone, leaving behind their tin sheds, corrugated roofs, even the cranes, to provide an exciting "working" setting for the leisure pursuits of prosperous Vancouverites. The kids love the Water Park playground and their Kids Only Market, selling toys, books and puppets. Adults prefer the Granville Island Brewery, pub and ultra-modern brewery where an afternoon half-hour tour will show you the (very good) lager being brewed. False Creek's south shore, also for long an industrial eyesore, has been transformed into a green and pleasant residential area.

English Bay

From its western tip at Point Grey back to False Creek, the bay's south shore offers an attractive series of beaches, parks and museums overlooking the Pacific. Point Grey provides a beautiful site for the campus of the University of British Columbia.

Museum of Anthropology

At 6393 Northwest Marine Drive is the magnificent building devoted to the culture of Canada's First Peoples. Arthur Erickson's 1972 masterpiece overlooking mountains and sea from the cliffs of Point Grey is a lateral design of glass and concrete beams in explicit tribute to the Northwest Coast Indians' wooden post-and-beam big-house. By way of comparison, two traditional Haida Indian cedarwood houses built in the 1930s can be seen in the ocean-front grounds near a group of ten imposing totem poles.

The museum's collections, subtly illuminated by intricate skylighting, include superb ceremonial masks and rattles, gold and silver jewellery, canoes and monumental artefacts such as 29

CREATION MYTHS

The First People reject scientific accounts of their origins as migrants from Asia in favour of their own Creation myths which postulate a permanent presence on the North American continent. Their frequently heard comment to Europeans states quite simply: "We've been here *all* the time." Certainly, Northwest Coast Indians feel their Creation myths—one featuring an enterprising raven flying between heaven and earth—are as valid as any proposed by the newcomers with their Garden of Eden.

giant cauldrons used in ceremonial feasts. The earliest versions of sculptures in wood, bone, stone or black argillite show that the same totemic motifs have endured since prehistoric times. The tradition continues to the present with the creation myth depicted in the massive yellow cedarwood *The Raven and the First Men* (1980) and other modern works by Haida sculptor Bill Reid.

The art of the Northwest Coast can be compared not only with that of other North American Indians but also with other Pacific Rim cultures, notably Japanese, Korean and Chinese. And instead of being hidden away in inaccessible cellars, the museum's vast reserves of artefacts from all around the world are open to the public in the Visible Storage Galleries.

Nitobe Memorial Gardens

A short walk through the campus south of the museum brings you to the Asian Centre and the otherworldly tranquillity of a classical Japanese garden, dedicated to scholar and diplomat Inazo Nitobe in 1960. A humpback bridge crosses a pond to a miniature island amid delicate Japanese maples, azaleas and other Oriental shrubbery, but also native pines, the whole arranged by Kyoto landscape artists. Visitors keep to the stone-lanterned paths meandering around quietly bubbling streams. A stepping stone path leads to a handsome traditional teahouse.

The Beaches

The seaward side of Marine Drive forms a chain of sandy beaches, popular for swimming, windsurfing and sailing, but long enough for them never to be too crowded. At the far western end beyond Point Grey, Wreck Beach is reserved for nude sun-bathing, but Locarno and Jericho Beaches are favourites for family swimming and water sports. Closer to downtown, Kitsilano ("Kits") is particularly popular for its heated saltwater swimming pool.

Other Museums

Immediately west of Burrard Bridge, Vanier Park's museum complex also includes a planetarium and space observatory.

The conical-roofed Maritime Museum celebrates the history of Vancouver's port. Pride of place goes to the two-masted schooner of the Royal Canadian Mounted Police, *Saint-Roch*. It circumnavigated the North American continent in 1944, through the Panama Canal and up the Pacific coast to the Arctic and through the Northwest Passage—the first vessel to tackle the route from west to east.

Vancouver Museum traces the city's history from the days of exploration and settlement to the momentous completion of the Canadian Pacific Railway and the early years of World War I.

Further west, Hastings Mill Museum (1575 Alma) presents a quaint collection of pioneer folklore in Vancouver's oldest surviving building. The Hastings Mill post office and general store of 1865 was brought here by barge in 1930.

The Canadian Craft Museum is housed downtown on the ground level of the Cathedral Place tower, 639 Hornby, displaying attractive craftwork—jewellery, basket-weaving, ceramics, bone- and wood-carving by Indians and Inuit, as well as by rural Canadians.

North Shore

The parks adjacent to the residential neighbourhoods of North and West Vancouver offer opportunities to taste the city's backdoors access to the BC wilderness.

Capilano River Park

Besides the cable car trip up Grouse Mountain for the view, the park is renowned for its spectacular century-old suspension bridge, 70 m (230 ft) above the canyon of the Capilano River. The river flows fast enough for some bone-shaking whitewater kayaking. There is also a salmon-hatchery and good hiking around Dog's Leg Pool.

Lynn Canyon Park

Directly north of the Second Narrows, the park's densely wooded hillsides have a more modest suspension bridge than Capilano's, but free of charge.

Lighthouse Park

The great attraction of West Vancouver's recreation park is that its pleasant forest trails culminate dramatically in granite boulders and cliffs—and a now disused lighthouse—at the Pacific Ocean entrance to English Bay.

Sea to Sky Highway

Once known as the Squamish Highway, the busy Route 99 north to the mountain resort of 31

Powwow with the Indians at Capilano River Park.

Whistler earns its new name with the spectacular views of sea and sky framed by soaring Douglas firs and the Coastal Mountains tumbling clear down to the Pacific. Beyond the ferry port of Horseshoe Bay, the range seems to have tossed a few peaks out in the waters of Howe Sound to form a hilly archipelago. Most attractive of the islands, Bowen Island is a favoured retreat for writers.

Britannia Beach

For over a century, until it was exhausted at the end of the 1970s, this was the centre of a hugely productive copper-mining area. The whole site has been transformed into the BC Museum of Mining where you can explore the tunnels, working machinery and the mill in which the ore was sluiced.

Shannon Falls

The waterfall, 335 m (1,098 ft) high, is the centrepiece of an attractive little park right beside the highway. Easily reached by a series of footbridges, it plunges over a cliff in an idyllic forest setting ideal for picnics.

Squamish

At the head of Howe Sound, the town is an important logging

centre, hosting the rumbustious World Lumberjack Competition every August in which logs get chopped, sawed, tossed and rolled for fun. The rest of the year, you can walk into the forest and see the same thing being done for money. "Squamish" means "mother of the wind" in the language of the Coast Salish, and indeed it does blow up a treat in the funnel formed at this end of Howe Sound, attracting shoals of windsurfers.

Garibaldi Provincial Park

Squamish provides a useful supply base for excursions into this vast expanse of forest, lakes, rivers and glaciers. Climbers head for challenging peaks like the park's highest, Wedge Mountain, 2,893 m (9,489 ft). But closer at hand on the west side of the park, a more modest and nonetheless invigorating one-day hike is possible along the well-marked hiking trail to the beautiful Garibaldi Lake.

Whistler

In the space of 30 years, the town has shot to top slot among North America's winter sports resorts, for amateurs and pros alike—a must on the World Cup skiing circuit—and is proving equally popular in summer. It started in 1914 with one little mountain lodge at Alta Lake, but remained strictly logging country until some ambitious entrepreneurs decided to develop the area as a candidate for the 1968 Winter Olympics. The bid failed but the skiing slopes continued to multiply. Originally known mundanely as London Mountain, the name had earlier been changed to evoke the piercing whistle of the marmots in its forests. Today, Whistler Mountain and its sister, Blackcomb Mountain, which opened to skiing in 1980, cater to a thriving centre of resort hotels, restaurants, bars, discos and smart shops. Thanks to the unpretentious style of British Columbians, there is a genuine village atmosphere. The area gets over 1,000 cm (400 inches) of snow each year and skiing continues into the summer months.

Even if you're not interesting in skiing, take the chair-lift up to the alpine meadows. For summer visitors, there are 33 km (20 miles) of hiking trails, mountain bikes to be rented, horseback riding, helicopter tours, tennis and four golf courses. Lost Lake has pleasant beaches for family swimming, while Alta Lake has good facilities for windsurfing and canoeing. The Whistler Summer Festival (July to mid-September) attracts top jazz, rock and world music groups, as well as the Vancouver Symphony Orchestra for open-air concerts.

33

VANCOUVER ISLAND
Victoria, South Coast, The Interior, Pacific Rim National Park, Inside Passage, Gulf Islands

As far as Europeans are concerned, Vancouver Island is where the story of British Columbia began. The west coast headquarters of the Hudson's Bay Company were set up in 1843 as the first supply centre for the gold rushes. Victoria was established as the provincial capital, and BC's prime timber forests were the first to be developed. The CPR's choice of Vancouver as its terminus halted Victoria's industrial development. This left the town with a tranquil charm that attracts thousands of visitors each year, particularly Americans. Victoria is an almost obligatory first stop before heading for the island's resorts and parks along the south and west coasts and bracing hikes through the interior's woods and mountains. People come from all over North America to fish offshore for Pacific salmon and halibut and in inland lakes and rivers for rainbow trout and small-mouth bass. The island's 7,000 Salish and Wakash Indians do their fishing well away from the tourist areas.

BC is governed from Victoria's turreted Parliament buildings.

The largest of the islands off North America's west coast, Vancouver Island extends some 460 km (287 miles) from north to south, with an average width of 80 km (50 miles). Mountainous and densely forested, it can claim the world's largest stand of commercial lumber. Most of its half million population is concentrated in the southern section around Victoria and along the east coast facing the mainland.

The charming little Gulf Islands, with their fishing villages and farming communities, are havens of tranquillity off the coast of Vancouver Island in the western waters of the Georgia Strait.

Victoria
BC's capital presents the Americans' idealized view of what a British town should be, and the Canadians' own deliciously distorted "memory" of what Britain once was. Victoria often seems to wave more Union Jacks than London. A mellow climate provides abundant sun, with just enough rain for flowers and shrubs to bloom all over the place. To accommodate the demand, English-style tea, scones and pastries are served from mid-

day to cocktail time. Even the finest hotels run into stiff competition from the splendid bed-and-breakfast boarding houses in comfortably renovated Victorian mansions set in obligatory flower gardens. And BC's disproportionately high number of Scottish immigrants fills the boutiques with every tartan plaid you can imagine. But all this gentility enjoys the un-British bonuses of the Pacific Ocean and mountains beckoning close at hand from the interior of Vancouver Island. Rudyard Kipling noted in Victoria the sleepy seaside atmosphere of Bournemouth or Torquay against a backdrop of the Himalayas.

The city centre is easily toured on foot, but you can also choose among the horse-drawn carriages lined up along the harbour front or the fleet of shiny red double-decker buses from London.

Empress Hotel

The first stop for many visitors, whether they are staying there or not, is this monumental hotel on Government Street overlooking the Inner Harbour. The Canadian Pacific Railway built it in 1908 as a grand consolation for not making Victoria its West Coast terminus; the well-heeled clients were ferried over from the mainland. As very British as the hotel wants its atmosphere to be, the architecture is in keeping with the railway company's taste for Renaissance roofing in the style of French Loire Valley châteaux.

Dress neatly if you want to take a look at the opulent décor of restaurants and bars, particularly the Tiffany-glass dome of the Crystal Lounge. For the privilege of partaking in the ritual afternoon high tea served in the spacious lobby lounge, you have to reserve in advance.

ISLAND HIGHLIGHTS

- **Botanical Beach**: fascinating tidal pools of marine life on island's south coast (p. 40).
- **Butchart Gardens**: exotic profusion of flowers and shrubs in the landfill of an exhausted limestone quarry (p. 40).
- **Cathedral Grove**: grand stand of giant Douglas firs (p. 42).
- **Empress Hotel**: Victoria's monument to genteel living and high tea (p. 36).
- **Long Beach**: endless stretch of fine sand for strolling and contemplating the Pacific (p. 44).
- **Saltspring Island**: artists' haven among Gulf Islands (p. 45).

VICTORIA

Skinner
John
Bay St.
Bay St.
Queens Ave.
ngford
Point Ellice Bridge
Rock Bay
Princess Ave.
Dowler
Central Park

Edward
Russel
Wilson
Alston
Bay St.
Tyee Rd.
Pembroke St.
Pembroke St.

Henry
Dundas
Victoria West Park
Discovery
Caledonia Ave.
Caledonia Ave.

William
Mary
Saghalie
Harbour Rd.
Store
Herald
Fiscard
Douglas St.
North Park St.
Balmoral Rd.
Vancouver

uimalt Rd.
Robert

Upper Harbour

Centennial
City Hall

Kimta Rd.
Johnson St. Bridge
Pandora Ave.

Wadding
Maritime Museum
Johnson St.

Victoria Harbour

Laurent Point
Inner Harbour
Yates St.
Blanshard St.
Yates St.

Shoal Point

Emily Carr Gallery
Wharf St.
View St.
View St.
Quadra St.
Fort St.

Fort St.
Broughton

Undersea Gardens
Courtney St.
Christ Church

nel t
Huron
Royal London Wax Museum
Kingston St.
Belleville St.
Government
Douglas St.
Court House
Burdett Ave.

Ontario St.
Michigan St.
Superior St.
Quebec Ave.
Car Museum
Crystal Gardens
McClure
Vancouver

St. Lawrence
Montreal
Simcoe St.
Ontario St.
Parliament Buildings
British Columbia Museum
Humboldt St.
Fairwield

MacDonald Park
Dock
Oswego
Michigan St.
Superior St.
Cook St.

Ogden nt Docks
Dallas Rd.
Niagara St.
Croft
Michigan St.
Toronto St.
Pendergast

San Jose
Boyd
Menzies St.
The Bridge Way
Oliphant
Park

Lewis
Menzies St.
Medina
Simcoe St.
The Circle
May St.
Linden

Rithet
South Turner
Government
Andrews
Douglas St.
Beacon Hill Park
Cook
Cambridge
Faithful St.

Dallas Rd.
Battery
Totem

Holland Point

N

0   500 m
0   500 yd

Juan de Fuca Strait

Dallas Rd.
Finlayson Point
Ross Bay

Parliament

More "British" in design than the Empress Hotel but sharing the same architect, Francis Rattenbury, the 1897 buildings make up a fanciful reminiscence of style elements from the Old Country: a main entrance with the neo-Romanesque archway of London's Natural Science Museum, a huge dome recalling St Paul's Cathedral—crowned by a statue of Captain George Vancouver—and flanking turrets that give the whole more the look of a town hall than a parliament. A tour inside reveals a debating chamber modelled on Westminster's House of Commons. More specifically Canadian are George Southwell's murals on the central rotunda celebrating British Columbia's first heroes—George Vancouver facing the Spanish at Nootka Sound, James Douglas setting up Fort Victoria for the HBC, the valiant workers who built it, and the keepers of law and order during the violent days of the 1858 gold rush. And Queen Victoria, of course, has her statue in the parliament grounds.

Royal British Columbia Museum

Just east of Parliament at 675 Belleville Street, this superbly designed museum uses the most modern hi-tech facilities to give a comprehensive view of life and culture in British Columbia. The First Peoples and Modern History galleries display the artefacts and everyday implements of the region's first Indian inhabitants and social history of the colonial

---

BLOOMING CRAZY

Victoria's citizens have taken the truly British passion for gardening to its ultimate limits. What began as a time-honoured colonial desire to impose a British way of life on newly conquered territory has become a consuming obsession. Even the street-lanterns have been hung with baskets of geraniums. In February, when other northerners stay snug and warm indoors, Victorians are outside for the Annual Flower Count. Armed with pocket calculators, they count every crocus and fruit-tree blossom and phone in their numbers to a municipal office, totalling in 1996 a record 4,220,401,563 flowers and blossoms. Like the Japanese taking their ritual outings to observe the new cherry blossom, this is the Victorians' endearingly potty way of saying farewell to winter. Prior, that is, to greeting the daffodils in March, tulips, rhododendrons, lilacs and dogwood in April and May, roses in June and the summer riot of begonias, gladiolas and chrysanthemums.

fur traders, fishermen, farmers, lumberjacks and factory-workers who followed. In the Natural History Gallery, among other displays of life from the Ice Age to the present day, the great Open Ocean exhibit simulates an underwater voyage in a submarine-like vessel from which to observe life in the ocean depths.

Thunderbird Park

Adjoining the museum, the park groups some important totem poles and Indian sculpture and a reconstructed Kwakiutl big-house. Also in the park is Helmcken House, built in 1852 and Victorian in every sense, preserved to display the furnishings in the prim and proper home of Fort Victoria's leading doctor, John Helmcken.

Maritime Museum

On Bastion Square, site of HBC's Fort Victoria headquarters, the old courthouse is now a museum devoted to merchant shipping. It exhibits navigational equipment and models of whalers, steamers and Hudson's Bay paddle-wheelers. A Victoria curiosity is Captain J.C. Voss's *Tilikum*, the three-sailed 40-ft dugout canoe he sailed around the world in 1901—three years from Victoria via Australia, Brazil and the Azores to the English seaside resort of Margate.

Two Galleries

The Emily Carr Gallery, 1107 Wharf Street, presents the works and memorabilia of the Victoria-born eccentric who painted landscapes and life among Vancouver Island Indians. (Her old boarding house is at 207 Government Street.) Out on Moss Street, the municipal Art Gallery has paintings by British Impressionist Walter Sickert (1860–1942) and French seascape artist Eugène Boudin (1824–1898).

Chinatown

Once infamous for its opium dens, the closest thing Victoria has to non-British exotica is North America's second-oldest Chinese community (after San Francisco). Behind the ornate Gate of Harmonious Interest, descendants of gold miners and railway workers live around the narrow Fan Tan Alley between Fisgard Street and Pandora. Their restaurants' steamed *dim sum* are first class.

The Gardens

The corner of Dallas Road and Douglas Street marks Kilometre Zero on the Trans Canada Highway, which ends, via a couple of ferries, 7,800 km (4,875 miles) east on another island at St John's, Newfoundland. It is also a good starting point to explore Victoria's love affair with flowers 39 and greenery, beginning with Beacon Hill Park's flower beds around formal gardens, but also wildflower meadows and groves of oak and cedar. North of the park, the Crystal Gardens conservatory offers tropical plants, exotic birds, snakes—and tea on the Upper Terrace.

The extravagant Butchart Gardens, best known of all, lie 22 km (13 miles) north of town. The English rose gardens, Japanese gardens, cypresses from Tuscany, fountains, streams, ponds and rockeries cover 20 ha (50 acres) in what was once the exhausted limestone quarry of cement magnate Robert Pim Butchart.

South Coast

Along a 107-km (66-mile) highway from Victoria via Sooke to Port Renfrew, the beaches are variously sand, pebbles or both, with spectacular views across the Juan de Fuca Strait to the state of Washington. The shoreline is very popular with surfers and windsurfers. Just inland are quiet woodlands and lakes for some good trout and bass fishing—and picnics. The resort towns offer plenty of excellent fish and seafood restaurants, together with well-appointed old fashioned bed-and-breakfast boarding houses, either overlooking the ocean or in their own lovingly landscaped gardens.

Sooke

The south coast's major resort makes a good base for exploring secluded coves along the seashore, hiking or horseback riding through the local nature reserve and along Galloping Goose Trail, past constantly changing landscapes of forest, cliffs, canyons, rivers, farmland and wildflower meadows. The Sooke Region Museum traces local history from the first settlers, T'Souke Indians, to the European lumberjacks, fishermen and farmers who followed. The major annual event is the All Sooke Day and Salmon Barbecue. Loggers from all over Canada gather for contests in axe-throwing, tree-chopping, double-man hand sawing, plus games for the kids, the whole followed by a gigantic salmon-bake over aromatic alder-wood fires. The grand event is on the third Saturday of July, but others on a smaller scale are held throughout the summer.

Botanical Beach

One of the island's most impressive seascapes is located just beyond the logging town of Port Renfrew. Sheltered by wooded cliffs, the broad shelf of sandstone rock is pocked with tidal pools revealing treasures of

Jenny Butchart turned her hubbie's quarry into a Garden of Eden.

marine life at low tide. (Look, but don't disturb.) The local newspaper—or the folk in Sooke or Port Renfrew—will give you the seasonal high and low tides timetable to know when to walk safely out among the pools. Botanical Beach is also the starting point of the new Juan de Fuca Marine Trail, a 49-km (30-mile) seashore hike east to China Beach.

The Interior
Beginning north of the port town of Nanaimo, Highway 4 from Parksville reveals some of BC's most beautiful countryside as it passes through forests and the rugged Mackenzie Mountains on its way to the Pacific coast.

Little Qualicum Falls
About 20 km (12 miles) from Parksville is an enchanting little park with a trail that follows the Qualicum river rapids rushing downhill through steep gorges and plunging waterfalls. A well-signposted walk takes you around the upper falls as it cascades into a ravine and continues down to the rocky gorge of the lower falls. The longer Wesley Ridge Trail is a more ambitious five-hour hike culminating in an exhilarating swim in Cameron Lake.

Cathedral Grove
The highway hugs the lake's southern shore to MacMillan Provincial Park and this noble stand of Douglas firs, the tallest trees in the Canadian forest. Named after 19th-century Scottish botanist David Douglas, the biggest here are 70 m (230 ft) tall with a trunk 2 m (6^{1}/$_{2}$ ft) wide. Many are over 300 years old, and the most ancient are said to date back to the 12th century. Cathedral Grove is a public donation by the MacMillan lumber company and paper manufacturer in exchange for the rights to log elsewhere in the forest. "Conscience money," say ecologists.

Port Alberni
At the head of the long Alberni Inlet, this is a good place to hire boats and equipment for ocean salmon and halibut fishing, and picnic supplies for the beach at Pacific Rim National Park. Its most popular attraction is the leisurely boat trip over to the Pacific coast aboard the little *MV Lady Rose*, leaving every morning from the Argyle Street dock. The highway west of town skirts Sproat Lake, reflecting the rugged peaks of the Mackenzie Mountains, with occasional bald slopes betraying the harm of over-logging.

Spared by the lumberjack's axe, giant Douglas firs in Cathedral Grove.

42

Pacific Rim National Park

Stretching 130 km (80 miles) along the west coast from Tofino to Port Renfrew, the park combines long, sandy beaches with coastal rainforest and mountains. Skilled surfers come here for the formidable breakers, fishermen for the chance to hook a salmon, most of all loafers to loaf. Grey whales and an occasional orca hang around the west coast and may be seen at Maquinna Marine Park, a 30-minute boat trip from Tofino. Others can be spotted by telescope from Long Beach vantage points such as Combers Beach, Schooners Cove and Quistis Point. Failing a whale, you may at least see a couple of smirking sea lions.

Long Beach

On the seaward side of Highway 4 where it turns north towards Tofino, Long Beach is just that— a 12-km (7-mile) expanse of fine windswept sand with a craggy backdrop of the Mackenzie Mountains. Scattered around are driftwood logs to sit on and stare out at the crashing ocean waves. Or you can peer at the marine life in the depths of a tidal pool among the rocks. An Information Centre on the highway publishes a Hiker's Guide to signposted trails leading to Half Moon Bay, Shorepine Bog and South Bay.

Tofino

This sleepy little fishing village today assembles a community of artists—avant-garde actors, poets and painters who came for the weekend and never left. Art galleries and an experimental theatre give you a glimpse of how they occupy their time. Hotel rooms here provide kitchen facilities for you to cook your fish-catch if it's too windy for a barbecue on the beach. From the harbour you can take a cruise out to Meares Island, covered in dense forest, and Hotspring Cove for a dip in the waterfall and four hot pools.

Broken Group Islands

Boats from Ucluelet or Bamfield take you out to this group of tiny, wonderfully unspoiled islands. They are much appreciated for scuba diving and canoeing around their secluded coves.

West Coast Trail

Starting just south of Bamfield, this coastal nature trail continues 77 km (48 miles) through rainforest and around rocky coves to Port Renfrew (maps from the Long Beach or Port Alberni information centres). It can take camping hikers a week to complete, but a day trip to the Pachena Lighthouse and back gives you a good sense of the diversity of the sea- and landscapes along the way.

Inside Passage

From Port Hardy at the north end of Vancouver Island, BC Ferries offer a 20-hour cruise up through the coastal islands to Prince Rupert. Besides the splendid scenery of fjords, waterfalls, glaciers and towering mountains, you may catch glimpses of seals, sea lions, dolphins, whales and a bald eagle or two.

Before making the return trip, try to visit Prince Rupert's Museum of Northern British Columbia for its excellent exhibits of Tsimshian Indian culture. Located in a native long house at Chatham Village, on the harbourfront, it traces 10,000 years of regional history.

Gulf Islands

The little Gulf Islands between Vancouver Island and the mainland are part of a sprawling archipelago extending south of the US border where they become the San Juan Islands. They provide a series of lovely resort areas for fishermen, sailors, hikers and nature lovers observing the abundant wildlife. Of the five main islands in the southern Gulf group, Saltspring and Galiano are the biggest, each with good restaurants and hotel or bed-and-breakfast accommodation. They are served by a good ferry service, from Tsawwassen on the mainland or, more frequently, from Swartz Bay north of Victoria.

Saltspring Island

The atmosphere here is much more relaxed than on big Vancouver Island. Painters, sculptors and potters have made it their home, and a major attraction is a tour of their studios—credit cards accepted. Their whereabouts are marked on island maps available at the ferry landings of Long Harbour, Vesuvius Bay or Fulford Harbour.

The main town is Ganges, with its colourful yachting harbour, galleries, craft-shops and some gourmet cuisine for the seafood and locally reared lamb and beef. Its Mahon Hall houses an annual summer Artcraft fair to celebrate the island's creativity. Drive—or hike—up Mount Maxwell for a beautiful view over Saltspring and the other Gulf Islands and south to the Cascade Mountains across the US border.

Galiano Island

Named after the Gulf Islands' first European explorer, Spanish captain Dionisio Galiano, this smaller, elongated island is popular for its marine nature reserves along the west coast, notably around Montague Harbour. Hikers head over to the east coast and make their way up to the beaches of Dionisio Point Provincial Park, in particular sandy Coon Bay. There are fine hilltop views from Galiano Bluffs and Mount Sutil. 45

INLAND

The region's first European explorers, as the names of the Fraser and Thompson rivers proclaim, followed the waterways to open up a cross-country route to the Pacific. To settle and industrialize the west, the CPR hacked its way along the route in the 19th century, followed by the Canadian National Railway (CNR) and Trans Canada Highway in the 20th. One of the most fascinating sights along the Fraser and Thompson Canyons today is to see the huge, seemingly endless freight trains of the rival railways passing each other by on opposite sides of the river on their way to and from the Pacific coast. (Their passenger services have been taken over by VIA Rail.)

Fraser and Thompson Canyons

The Trans Canada Highway east out of Vancouver follows the Fraser River as it turns north to meet the Thompson River and then follows the latter over to the transport junction town of Kamloops. The mighty waterways and awesome canyons towering over swirling rapids provide an exhilarating journey of discovery through landscapes alternating mountain, rainforest and semi-arid desert.

The route charts vital elements in the life of Western Canada: Pacific salmon swim up the two rivers far inland to spawn their young, which then follow the same course back to the ocean; Interior Salish Indians, drawn by the abundant fish, have made their home in the river valleys—still present in its remoter parts.

Hope

The town commands the valley where the jagged peaks of the Cascade Mountains begin to close in on the Fraser River and its Coquihalla tributary—the mountain range extends south of the US border into Washington. Before heading upriver in the 1858 gold rush, ironic prospectors with a literary turn of mind are said to have taken the town's name from a famous line in Dante's *Inferno*: "Abandon all hope, ye who enter here." Endowed with a charmingly rickety folklore museum on Water Street, Hope serves as a base for canoeing and fishing expeditions into the pretty Kawkawa Lake Provincial Park just north of town.

Yale

Hemmed in by ever narrowing cliffs that turn Fraser Valley into Fraser Canyon, this is as far 47 upstream as cargo vessels from Vancouver can get before the rapids begin. It was founded as the terminus for HBC's stern-wheelers to pick up their pelts—the boats' mooring rings can still be seen on the river bank at low water. Hereafter, the Fraser is strictly for canoes and white-water rafting. Now just a tiny logging community with barely a couple of hundred inhabitants, Yale had its moment of glory in 1858 when the gold rush made it Canada's biggest town west of Ontario. Indeed, throughout the west, only San Francisco out-numbered its 20,000 prospectors, suppliers and hangers-on.

Thirty years later, the CPR brought another surge of pros-perity by choosing Yale as its construction depot and goods yard—until it was transferred to Vancouver. On Douglas Street, Yale Museum tells the full story.

Hell's Gate

Some 20 km (12 miles) north of Yale, the fast-flowing river be-comes a veritable torrent rushing through a narrow gorge between cliffs 180 m (590 ft) high and just 40 m (131 ft) across, the perfect natural fish-trap for the Salish to catch their salmon. With the roil-ing waters at this point 60 m (196 ft) deep, it also looked like a

---

SALMON: THE UPS AND DOWNS

A salmon's life is not easy. It spawns in a stream near enough to a lake for the hatched young or small fry, as it's known, to take its first swim to the lake. Feeding on water fleas, it will grow to about 10 cm (4 in) before venturing towards the river. After a year or two, having become a smolt, it is ready to head for the ocean, often more than 1,500 km (nearly 1,000 miles) away. Only one in 20 makes it. In the sea, it fattens up for three summers on shrimp, growing big enough to call itself a real salmon, weighing over 3 kg (7 lb). Then it goes home to spawn. If it's lucky. At the Fraser estuary, for instance, the commercial fisheries are waiting with their nets. Survivors make their way upstream to the exact same spawning ground where they were born four years before. By late autumn, after a journey of perhaps 50 days' non-stop swimming, the female scours a nest in the gravel with her tail and lays some three to four thousand eggs to be sprayed by sperm from the male. Battered by their fights with the rocky rapids and perhaps narrow escapes from predators, human and otherwise, the exhausted parents die within ten days, leaving the young fry to hatch in the spring and begin the new cycle.

Feeling lazy? Try whitewater rafting and let the current do all the hard work.

hellish death-trap to fur trader Simon Fraser on his way down-river in 1808. Luckily, the Indians could help him manoeuvre his canoe past the rapids along a tee-tering ropeway of creeper lashed to the canyon wall. Today, the Air Tram cable car makes things a lot easier for visitors to get right down to the rapids. A restaurant at the cable car lower terminus serves sockeye salmon, grilled or poached.

These salmon nearly disap-peared in 1914 because of an eco-logical disaster brought on by the Canadian National Railway's rock blasts. They blocked the passage—and reduced the annual catch by 90 per cent—until new steel-and-concrete channels were built for them 30 years later. The salmon are back and the Salish have moved upstream to do their fishing with dip-nets on long rods from rocky ledges or log-plat-forms hugging the canyon wall.

Lytton

The town lies at the confluence of the Fraser River, 1,370 km (856 miles) long, and its Thompson tributary, 489 km (305 miles) long but scarcely less formidable. Lytton likes to be known as the Rafting Capital of Canada. Cer-tainly, this is the place to rent a raft, a canoe or kayak and tackle 49 the swirling whitewater rapids on either of the two rivers. Over an embankment on Highway 12, north of town, you can discern the confluence in action as the lime-coloured Thompson flows beside the silvery waters of the Fraser until the two blend for their journey to the ocean.

Around Kamloops

Following the Thompson Valley north and east to the transportation centre of Kamloops, the Trans Canada Highway passes through arid desert-like country. The brown rock-strewn landscape of sagebrush and other dry scrub has prompted people here to claim it is a northerly last gasp of the Mojave Desert. This affinity with the American Southwest is enhanced by the many cattle ranches around Kamloops. The town's museum has a fine exhibit on the Shuswap Indians.

Squilax

Anyone in the region in October can witness here the dramatic salmon run of thousands of fish triumphantly reaching their spawning grounds. On the Trans Canada Highway east of Kamloops, the Squilax turn-off takes you to the junction of Adams River and Shuswap Lake to see the waters turn crimson with sockeye salmon making their amazing final dash for home.

Okanagan Valley

Sun-drenched orchards and vineyards are not what you expect of British Columbia. Yet that is exactly what greets you along the valley nestling between the Fraser Canyon's Cascade Mountains and the Rockies. The brilliant springtime display of blossoms here forces the admiration even of visitors from Victoria. Every summer, cheerful resort towns and campgrounds welcome thousands of Canadian and American tourists for the water sports along the sandy beaches of Okanagan's elongated lake and the after-dark entertainment in the bars. They come, too, for the valley's apricots, peaches, plums,

---

FRUITFUL MISSION

In 1859, two Catholic missionaries, Fathers Charles Pandosy and Pierre Richard, came to spread the good word to Okanagan Valley. Their sermons were given a polite hearing by the largely Protestant community, but they really stirred up enthusiasm with the apple trees and grapevines they planted on their little estate. The Father Pandosy Mission church and farm buildings have been understandably preserved as a local monument at 3685 Benvouline Road, southeast of Kelowna's centre.

cherries, apples and pears—find out the current crop from the local newspaper's pay-for-what-you-pick advertisements.

The Okanagan Wine Festival is held in early October—tastings galore, along with gourmet dining, picnics, dancing, jazz bands, art exhibitions and a family grape stomp competition. And all year round, in an area boasting Canada's warmest winters, you can visit individual vineyards for tastings. In recent years, with refined modernized techniques, the region's sandy soil, abundant sun and just the right early autumn chill have produced BC reds and whites that compete with honours in international competition with the best wines of Europe and California.

Kelowna

The valley's bouncing "capital" is the gateway to the best orchards and vineyards, many of them across the lake at Westbank and Peachland. Among the better-known vineyards that welcome visitors are Quails' Gate and Mission Hill at Westbank and Calona and Gray Monk immediately north of Kelowna. The City Park's public beach is popular for family bathing, while Rotary Beach south of town attracts the windsurfers. At 470 Queensway Avenue, Kelowna Museum and Art Gallery trace the region's story from prehistoric dinosaurs to the life of Interior Salish Indians and European pioneers, along with exhibitions of modern painters and sculptors. A new Wine Museum has opened on Ellis Street.

Penticton

With an average of 10 hours a day, it claims more summer sunshine than Honolulu. This and the countless bars and discos should be enough to justify, for the raver fraternity, the town's name in Salish, *pen tak tin*, meaning "place to stay forever"—or at least all night. The social season begins with a Blossom Festival in April, followed by a more boisterous Peach Festival in July. The South Okanagan Art Gallery adds a genteel touch with some of the valley's best art shows.

The most enjoyable of Penticton's beaches is in fact 4 km (2½ miles) south of town, out at Skaha Lake.

Osoyoos

The valley's hot spot is down on the US border, a little patch of real desert with coyotes, lizards, rattlesnakes and horned toads creeping around the cactus and sagebrush. Not surprising, then, that the fruit grown here is bananas and pomegranates. The town also has a pleasant lake for swimming.

51

Rocky Mountains

In all of Western Canada there is no more grandiose landscape than the Rocky Mountains straddling the BC-Alberta border. North America's great mountain range stretches at its greatest estimate over 4,800 km (3,000 miles) from central New Mexico up through Canada to northwest Alaska—though Canadian geologists insist the Rockies end in the Yukon. The Canadian Rockies extend west across the trench formed by the Columbia, Fraser and Peace rivers to include the Selkirk, Purcell, Monashee and Cariboo Mountains. The highest Canadian peak is BC's Mount Robson, 3,954 m (12,973 ft).

BRITISH COLUMBIA ROCKIES

Mount Revelstoke NP, Glacier NP, Yoho NP, Kootenay NP

The national parks of the Rocky Mountains have an abundance of wildlife, principally in the remoter parts of the forests but also occasionally venturing over mountain paths or even crossing the highway right in front of your vehicle, so watch out. Porcupine, bighorn sheep, mountain goats, deer and especially elk are not uncommon and nothing to be afraid of. More rarely seen are moose, coyote, wolves and bears, black or grizzly.

The snow-clad summit of Mt Robson, highest peak of the Canadian Rockies.

Efficiently run, the national and provincial parks are equipped with hotels, camping grounds, hiking trails and other summer and winter sports facilities. The park information offices can provide a useful leaflet explaining how to deal with the problem of bears.

Mount Revelstoke National Park

The Trans Canada Highway to Mount Revelstoke follows the Eagle River from the salmon spawning grounds east of Kamloops, through the Monashee Mountains. Eagle Pass was the route chosen by the Canadian

Pacific Railway for its final stretch of track to breach the mighty barrier of the Rockies. The railway and highway skirt the southern edge of the Revelstoke park which, undisturbed by hotels or towns inside its boundaries, is a great favourite with fishermen and bird-watchers.

Craigellachie

Beside the highway some 25 km (15 miles) east of Shuswap Lake, a slab of granite marks the spot where North America's first transcontinental railway joined up tracks laid over 4,800 km (3,000 miles) from the Atlantic to the Pacific. It was here that Donald Smith, a major CPR shareholder, drove in the celebrated Last Spike at precisely 9.22 a.m. on November 7, 1885. It is told that a few minutes earlier, when Smith's flowing white beard got in the way of his aim, the first hammer-swipe had knocked a penultimate spike askew. Named after a remote village in the Scottish Grampians where Smith grew up, Craigellachie was a train station and water fuelling stop until the 1950s. Now there's just a little park with gift shop and picnic tables.

Three Valley Gap, 19 km (12 miles) west of Revelstoke, is an ever-increasing re-creation of a pioneer settlement near the ghost of an 1880s mining town.

Revelstoke

The town enjoyed a golden era in the CPR's early years and still has some fine Victorian and Edwardian buildings to show for it, notably an imposing domed courthouse not far from the railway track. A modern Railway Museum celebrates the good old days with the grand freight Engine No. 5468 and, for executives on fat expense-accounts, Business Car No. 4 built in the 1920s. Revelstoke descendants of railway labourers now have an easier time of it running a couple of good Chinese restaurants.

Mount Revelstoke

Just east of town, exit the Trans Canada Highway to take the winding Summit Road all the way to the top of the mountain, 1,942 m (6,370 ft), the only peak in Canada offering motorists such a lazy climb. There is a fine view over the Illecillewaet and Columbia river valleys between the Monashee Mountains. Hikers have the choice of 65 km (40 miles) of clearly marked trails—maps available from park headquarters at 301B Third Street West in downtown Revelstoke. Three easy walks are the short Giant Cedars and Skunk Cabbage boardwalks, and the paved Meadows-in-the-Sky Trail, from the summit through sub-alpine meadows covered by snow for three-quarters of the year. On the way, you may see elk, moose, mountain sheep and, with luck at a safe distance, black bear. Birds to watch for are golden eagle, blue grouse or grey jay. With a permit from the park HQ, fishermen head for Eva and Jade lakes for the trout—rainbow, broke, brown and cut-throat—or bass, char and whitefish.

Glacier National Park

The skyline is chillingly stark and jagged, an awesome sight that all but the most intrepid hikers, climbers and cross-country skiers prefer to see from the comfort of their car as they drive through on the Trans Canada Highway. The park counts over 400 glaciers and 15 per cent of it is under a permanent blanket of ice or snow. The Purcell Mountains, south of the little town of Golden, are a centre for heli-skiing in remote areas such as the Bugaboos.

Rogers Pass

Locals say it rains eight days a week at the pass named after Major A.B. Rogers, who discovered it in 1882 as a way through the treacherous Selkirk Mountains for the CPR. At an altitude of 1,330 m (4,362 ft), it also proved the most formidable obstacle to be cleared in completing the Trans Canada Highway in 1962. The railway track has since

---

YOUNG ROCKIES

The extravagant landscapes—recalling jagged sawteeth, solitary Egyptian pyramids or crenellated battlements of Europe's medieval castles—derive from the mountains being, in geological terms, relatively "young". Formed by shudders in the earth's crust scarcely 60 million years ago, the peaks have been eroded to reveal ancient crystalline cores flanked by gigantic slabs of sedimentary rock.

---

been abandoned but now marks an interesting and easy hiking trail, just over a kilometre either way.

Yoho National Park

This is quite simply one of the Rockies' prettiest parks. *Yoho* is a Cree Indian word for "amazement", and that is not far from the reaction you may have in contemplating the scenic beauty of its waterfalls, lakes and mountains along the Kicking Horse and Yoho rivers. Its eastern boundary rises to the Continental Divide, the watershed from which the rivers run either west to the Pacific or east and north to Hudson's Bay and the Arctic.

Wapta Falls

Entering the park from the lumber town and railway depot of 55

Cosy cabin on the shores of O'Hara Lake. Who needs a palace to live in?

Golden, a turn-off to the south takes you to the Wapta Falls hiking trail. This easy 20-minute walk takes you to a lovely cascade near which a pack horse kicked explorer James Hector in the chest and inspired the name of the Kicking Horse River and the notorious pass on the east side of the park.

Emerald Lake

For many, the discreet beauty of its tranquil, truly emerald waters located in the middle of the park makes this lake infinitely more enchanting than its more celebrated rival, Lake Louise, over the Alberta border. Its signposted road turns north off the Trans Canada Highway, just west of the parkside town of Field. The road leads first to an impressive Natural Bridge in the woods, a solid granite rock through which the Kicking Horse River's torrential stream has worn its channel, with a picnic area for you to enjoy the spectacle. Emerald Lake itself has some delightful rambles around its shores, in and out of the woods with frequent glimpses of wildlife of the more peaceful variety—mostly porcupines and beaver. With one lodge of elegantly timbered cabins, the lake also offers good facilities for canoeing and horseback riding.

Kicking Horse Pass

Though it may be snowbound until mid-June, the steep and narrow Yoho Valley road winds 13 km (8 miles) through pine forests beside the Yoho River to give you some of the park's best sights on the way.

Just south of the confluence of the clear blue Yoho and silted Kicking Horse rivers is the Upper Spiral Tunnel. With luck, you'll see trains coming in and out of one of two tunnels hewn out of Cathedral Mountain. They form a figure 8—an astute engineering solution to diminish the gradient over Kicking Horse Pass from a hazardous 4.5 per cent to a manageable 2.2 per cent. Sometimes as many as eight locomotives, four pushing and four pulling, are needed to get one great eastbound lumber freight-train through the tunnel.

Takakkaw Falls

At the far end of the Yoho Valley road, the plunging waterfalls are an exhilarating sight—*takakkaw* means "magnificent", fair comment. Pouring from the outflow of the Daly Glacier, the free-falling waters of 254 m (833 ft) make this cascade one of the highest in Canada. Unlike most waterfalls, Takakkaw is at its best in the heat of high summer when the glacier ice is melting profusely. You get a great view of the glacier itself along the Highline hiking trail that starts near the Whiskey Jack youth hostel.

O'Hara Lake

South of the Trans Canada Highway, this lake nestles against the western slopes of Mount Victoria, 3,465 m (11,368 ft), and Mount Lefroy 3,424 m (11,230 ft), two of the mountains that form the Great Divide. The hikes here are more perhaps more strenuous than those at Emerald Lake but the scenery more than repays the effort, notably along the Odaray Plateau and up to Lake Oesa.

Kootenay National Park

Immediately south of Yoho and west of Banff, this appealingly tranquil park nestling up against the Continental Divide is relatively off the beaten track for visitors to the Rockies. The park's attractions can be enjoyed on a day trip along Highway 93 as it winds some 100 km (62 miles) between the Trans Canada Highway and the western exit at Radium Hot Springs. The more properly designated Kutenai Indians, who left their name on the river along which they settled, now occupy land in southeastern BC, northern Idaho and northern Montana. They are historic enemies of the Blackfoot.

57

Vermilion Pass

The northern entrance is at the Continental Divide's watershed, 1,637 m (5,369 ft). You can still see the aftermath of a huge forest fire that swept through the area in 1968. Interpretive panels on the short Fireweed Trail circuit explain how the forest is regenerating with new shrubs and wildlife and above all sturdy lodgepole pines that positively thrive in the special conditions of a burn.

Marble Canyon

A short walk over log footbridges takes you to one of the more colourful canyons in the Rockies. The blue glacial meltwater of Tokkum Creek and grey limestone cliffs set off by green shrubs clinging to the rockface make a handsome setting for the climactic waterfall roaring into the gorge 37 m (121 ft) below.

Paint Pots

The Vermilion River at this point is foaming white, but there is plenty of red, orange and mustard-yellow in bubbling pools left by iron-rich minerals. A 10-minute walk will get you there. Plains Indians used to cross the Rockies to gather the ochre pigment from these pools for their ritual bodypaint and rock murals. In the 1920s, the ochre was mined for paint manufacturers in Calgary.

Mount Wardle

Some 40 km (25 miles) from the park's northern entrance, scores of mountain goats come down the slopes in the spring with their new-born kids to lick for the minerals in the clay at the side of the highway. These bearded fellows are the Kootenay Park's emblem.

Kootenay Valley Viewpoint

A huge lay-by here allows you to see or capture on film a superb panorama across the Kootenay River and the snowcapped peaks of the Mitchell and Vermilion mountains.

Olive Lake

The little sparkling green lake at the top of Sinclair Pass, 1,486 m (4,874 ft) makes a charming picnic area. A pleasant boardwalk is laid out as an informative nature trail along the lake shore.

Sinclair Canyon

Just inside the park's western entrance, the canyon provides access to the pools for the nearby spa town of Radium Hot Springs. Tiny quantities of radium in the 45°C (113°F) open-air pools are believed by its 4,000 annual visitors to have therapeutic value. A little further are the soaring iron-rich cliffs of the Redwall Fault which gives its name to the nearby Redstreak Mountain.

ALBERTA ROCKIES

Banff National Park, Icefields Parkway, Jasper National Park

In 1885, two years after the Canadian Pacific Railway reached Banff, the government realized that this beautiful land had to be protected in the face of the potential ravages of mass transportation and industrial expansion. When three railway workers accidentally came across what became known as the Cave and Basin hot springs, they vied with their company for rights to exploit this clearly lucrative region. The federal government promptly stepped in to create on the Alberta side of the Rockies the first and indisputably still best-known of Canada's national parks.

Banff National Park

It includes within its 6,641 sq km (2,564 sq miles) of parkland two truly breathtaking highways through forest, lakes and mountains—the Bow Valley Parkway linking the grand resorts of Banff itself and Lake Louise and, continuing north, the Icefields Parkway that it shares with Jasper National Park. For hikers, mountain-bikers and horseback riders, and for winter cross-country skiers, there are some 1,500 km (930 miles) of marked trails. For nature-lovers, Banff's park boasts the whole panoply of Rockies wildlife: elk, moose, bighorn sheep, mountain goat, coyotes and wolves, black and grizzly bears.

Banff

This isn't a town that became a resort, it's a resort that became a town. Overlooked by lovely Castle Mountain, it began as a place for wealthy travellers, some of whose elegant Edwardian villas and cottages can be seen on a stroll along Lynx, Beaver and Buffalo streets north of the Bow River. Today it is particularly popular with Japanese adepts of hot springs spas, among them lots of honeymoon couples wandering around hand in hand. The main street, Banff Avenue, has a plethora of souvenir shops, boutiques and restaurants, some of them picturesquely housed in the old Cascade Dance Hall.

There are several museums worth a look: the old Banff Park and Natural History museums on Banff Avenue present exhibits on the park's wildlife, flora and geology; the Whyte Museum on Bear Street traces in photographs the history of the resort; and Luxton Museum south of the river on Birch Avenue is devoted to the life, weapons and crafts of Cree and Assiniboine Indians. 59

Banff Springs Hotel

Declared a National Historic Site, this refurbished Victorian neo-Gothic palace completed in 1888 can justifiably be considered a monument in its own right. The flagship of CPR's luxury resort-hotels is certainly worth a tour. Even if you are not staying there, splash out on the exorbitant high tea in the lounge overlooking the Bow River and then wander down to the nearby Bow Falls.

The Hot Springs

Up on Sulphur Mountain along Cave Avenue, 3 km (2 miles) west of the hotel, see the original Cave and Basin springs which launched the resort. The sulphurous pools are not currently available for bathing, but you can visit the cave explored by the brothers William and Tom McCardell and Frank McCabe, who were in fact looking for gold, not hot water. The springs had, of course, long been known to Assiniboine Indian hunters for soothing their tired bones and other ills. However, not even the railway workers understood their full commercial potential—they sold their rights to the Canadian government for a mere $900 (which now might get you a suite in the Banff Springs Hotel). Bathers seeking to take the waters head south to the Upper Hot Springs at the end of Mountain Avenue. One pool has hot water rising to 42°C (107°F) in summer for soaking, another a comfortably warm 27°C (80°F) for swimming.

Cable Car Rides

Known as gondolas here, cable cars glide up Sulphur Mountain from the Upper Hot Springs on Mountain Road to a great view from the top, 2,255 m (7,396 ft), and to two easy walks—the Summit Ridge Trail and the Vista Trail up to Sanson Peak. Or drive 18 km (11 miles) southwest of town to take the Sunshine Gondola up to the new Sunshine Village resort. From there, for the same price, the Standish Chairlift continues on up to the Continental Divide, where a marker at 2,430 m (7,970 ft) defines the Alberta-BC border. Walk back to the resort through Sunshine Meadows.

Minnewanka Loop

Just east of Banff town, this circuit around three lakes, of which the long meandering Minnewanka is the park's biggest, makes a pleasant day trip. You'll have good opportunities for boating, scuba diving and bird-watching in the summer, or cross-country skiing in the winter. You will also

The sheer serenity of Moraine Lake.

pass the ghost town of Bankhead, where coal was mined for the CPR from 1903 to 1922.

Bow Valley Parkway

Starting 6 km (nearly 4 miles) west of Banff town, this route to Lake Louise (Highway 1A) is much more relaxed and prettier than the more direct but more crowded Trans Canada Highway. On the way, stop off to hike the marked trail along the fast flowing creek through Johnston Canyon. A perfectly manageable catwalk has been built into the side of the canyon for you to walk above the rapids to two waterfalls, just over 1 km to the lower, 2.7 km (1.6 miles) to the upper falls. If you do take the Trans Canada, you are compensated with a good view east across Bow River to the battlemented silhouette of Castle Mountain, 2,862 m (9,390 ft).

Lake Louise

The sheer scenic magnificence of its setting overcomes whatever anybody can say about the overcrowded tourist-trap that Lake Louise and its big Château hotel have undoubtedly become. The lake is a deeper turquoise blue than any picture-postcard could conjure up. Known to Assiniboine Indians as the Lake of Little Fishes, it was renamed after one of Queen Victoria's many little daughters. Indeed, the lake is an outflow of Victoria Glacier, brilliantly mirrored in the waters along with the pine forests and snowy peaks of Mount Fairview and Mount Whyte.

Around the Lake

Take advantage of the area's many delightful hiking trails, easy along the lake shore and only a little more strenuous over to neighbouring Lake Agnes, with the bonus of a pretty shoreside teahouse. The trail continues a kilometre to the Little Beehive overlooking Bow Valley or, same distance but slightly higher, over to the Big Beehive. Another popular lakeshore hike, just over 5 km (3 miles), takes you to the Plain of the Six Glaciers—and another teahouse. For the footsore, the Lake Louise Gondola wafts you up for an eagle's-eye view from the slopes of Mount Whitehorn. The cable car station is near Lake Louise Village, 4½ km (3 miles) from the lake and little more than a shopping mall which serves as supply base for hikers and campers.

Moraine Lake

At the end of the mountain road running 14 km (8 miles) south of Lake Louise, this is visually a close rival, with its star attraction on the way being the sawtooth silhouette of the Valley of the

Ten Peaks. One of the most popular hikes from the lake takes you up through enchanting alpine meadows to Larch Valley.

Icefields Parkway

On the map, the road along the eastern edge of the Canadian Rockies' spine, the Continental Divide, is just Highway 93. But the 230-km (143-mile) route from Lake Louise to Jasper was rightly known by the fur traders as "Wonder Trail". Its matchless views encompass misty waterfalls, enchanting lakes and canyons, and above all the dazzling glaciers that have given it its latterday name, and whose outflows feed mighty rivers heading to the oceans. The highway does not follow the most direct path, but has been built to seek out the area's finest sights around the mountains and through the more spectacular passes. Allow plenty of time—at least a day—for walks to the more dramatic sights just off the road. For hikers, horseback riders and campers, it deserves a week. In any case, slow down to see—and not run over—the local wildlife, even an occasional moose.

Crowfoot Glacier

This glacier, 33 km (20 miles) from the junction with the Trans Canada Highway near Lake Louise, earned its name a century ago when the foot still had three "toes" of ice cascading over a cliff. Spilling out of a cleft that it has worn in the mountains, it has broken off one toe, but the great layer of ice remaining is 50 m (164 ft) thick, a formidable sight.

Peyto Lake

A signpost at the parkway's highest point—Bow Summit, 2,088 m (6,850 ft) above sea level—leads to a charming 20-minute walk up to a splendid lookout over the glacial lake. Often frozen white until well into June, it is a beautiful blue-green in high summer and surrounded in July and August by meadows of wild flowers.

Mistaya Canyon

Just 15 minutes' walk from the roadside, the Mistaya river quickly narrows into a twisting canyon marked by rounded potholes and a natural arch worn into the rockface.

Saskatchewan River Crossing

Long before the supermarket, restaurant and filling station were built here, this was the point at which fur traders and other adventurers stopped to rest before crossing the Continental Divide. It is in fact the confluence of three rivers, Howse, Mistaya and North Saskatchewan, and it was here that David Thompson took his

canoe into the Howse on his westward journey of discovery in 1807. (The eastbound highway bears his name.)

Parker's Ridge

At Kilometre 117, hikers can enjoy a fine walk up a short but steeply winding path to a ridge looking down over alpine meadows to the Sakatchewan Glacier. This vast expanse of ice is the source of the great North Saskatchewan river that links up with the waterways in the prairies to flow into the Hudson's Bay.

Columbia Icefield

Just inside Jasper National Park west of the Parkway, the Columbia's eight glaciers cover an area of 325 sq km (125 sq miles). Three of them are visible from the road—the Athabasca, Dome and Stutfield. The Icefield Centre provides excellent information and films, but this is the place to get out on to the ice. Put on some good thick-soled shoes and take a stroll on the Athabasca Glacier— or hop on a "SnoCoach". The glacier is receding and leaving moraine rock rubble in its wake; in the 19th century, it extended to the other side of the Parkway.

The Sunwapta River takes the plunge over a cliff into a deep limestone canyon.

Sunwapta Falls

A side-road off west of the Parkway leads you over to the impressive canyon that the falls have cut from the Sunwapta Valley into the broader Athabasca Valley 55 m (180 ft) below. *Sunwapta* is an Indian word meaning "turbulent waters".

Athabasca Falls

At Kilometre 199, an easily negotiated boardwalk takes you around the thunderous cascade that plunges into a deep gorge to launch the Athabasca River on its eastward journey through the town of Jasper and down into the prairies.

Jasper National Park

With an area of 10,878 sq km (4,200 sq miles), the park would be big enough to swallow its Rocky Mountain rivals, Banff, Yoho and Kootenay, but its northerly location has given it a more discreet profile. In fact, as you may have already seen in part along the Icefield Parkway, the backwoods attractions are great, the wildlife is abundant, and the sports facilities for hikers and campers in summer, and for skiers in winter, are first-class.

In the backcountry wilderness, the trails stretching over 1,000 km (625 miles) are rated among the best in North America. Shorter trails for casual ramblers are less numerous, but walks around the lakes just outside the town of Jasper can be very enjoyable.

Jasper

First called Fitzhugh, the town was renamed in 1913 after Jasper Hawes, agent of the North West Company who set up a fur-trading post here on the Athabasca River a century earlier. The town is now a major Rockies depot for the Canadian National Railway. Despite the imposing Jasper Park Lodge maintaining the classical tradition of luxury resort hotels, Jasper's small-town atmosphere still makes it seem more of a pioneering outpost than a modern holiday resort.

The little Jasper Yellowhead Museum on Pyramid Lake Road combines an art gallery with exhibits on the town's history.

The Lake Walks

There are half a dozen delightful lakes within 10 km (6 miles) of town, easily reachable on foot or bicycle. They have sandy beaches or grassy meadows to picnic on and facilities for canoeing, boating and windsurfing.

The most popular beaches are close at hand on Edith and Annette lakes. To the northwest are two pleasant excursions to Pyramid and Patricia lakes. The latter includes the Cottonwood

marshes offering good opportunities for bird-watching and spotting beaver, deer and elk.

Jasper Tramway

Just 7 km (4 miles) south of town, the cable car takes you up to fine views from Whistlers Mountain, including a glimpse of the highest peak in the Rockies, Mount Robson, 3,954 m (12,973 ft). The view is even better for those who dress warmly for the one-hour hike on to the Whistlers summit, a mere 2,466 m (8,090 ft).

Maligne Valley

Taking in a canyon, two lakes and plentiful wildlife, this is undoubtedly the park's most popular excursion, 11 km (6 miles) east of town. The facilities include boating, whitewater rafting, fishing, horseback riding and guided hiking tours. It got its "evil" name when being cursed by a Belgian Catholic priest, Father Pierre Jean de Smet, struggling to cross it with his horses in 1846.

Maligne Canyon

The canyon is a geologist's delight, both for the peculiar effects that erosion has caused in its hollows and ledges, but also for the many fossils to be found here (and surrendered to park authorities). The river plunges 23 m (75 ft) into a gorge where

Perfectly framed and hauntingly beautiful, Spirit Island in Maligne Lake.

the water can go down to a depth of 50 m (164 ft). Though the canyon narrows in places to just 2 m (6 ft), many who have tried to jump across are buried in Jasper cemetery.

Medicine Lake

Fed in spring and summer by the Maligne River and subterranean springs, the lovely lake, a favourite waterhole for bighorn sheep, mysteriously disappears in the autumn. The water is siphoned off into underground caves and channels like plug-holes in a bathtub, the springs freeze in winter and gush out again only in the spring thaw.

Maligne Lake

Its dimensions are impressive: 22 km (13 miles) long and 97 m (318 ft) deep. It boasts a superb backdrop of towering peaks, Mount Samson, 3,082 m (10,112 ft) on the eastern shore and Mount Brazeau 3,471 m (11,388 ft) looming above the Coronet Glacier at the far end. Boat cruises out to Spirit Island are a sheer joy. The lake is rich in fish—pike, whitefish, trout and char—but anglers with a permit must fish without bait or lead weights and observe maximum catch and possession limits of only two game fish on any one day.

67

Alberta and the Prairie Provinces

Wealth in the 20th century from oil and natural gas has made Alberta disarmingly brash and brassy. Alberta doesn't lay claim—the Rockies apart—to the same kind of awe-inspiring beauties that are the pride of its western neighbour over in BC. What Albertans really rather relish are the almost intimidating wide open spaces of the rolling, treeless, short-grass prairies and the arid, rough, tough Badlands. These are the distinctive features of southern Alberta stretching away from Calgary—the land, as its boosters happily proclaim, of dinosaurs, buffalo, coyotes, rattlesnakes, horned toads and pronghorn antelope. Further south towards the US border, the ranches rear cattle producing Canada's best steaks and prime rib.

CALGARY
Downtown, Fort Calgary, Prince's Island,
Calgary Stampede, Head-Smashed-in Buffalo Jump

Apart from its oilfields, central Alberta around Edmonton—what the province likes to call its Heartland—is fertile parkland and farming country, the western end of Canada's great wheat belt, irrigated by the North Saskatchewan river basin. In a province that is unashamedly mercantile, it is not surprising that Edmonton's best-known monument is its outsize shopping mall.

The population is 77 per cent urban and only 9 per cent of the rest are farmers. A large majority is of British extraction, but there are important minorities of Germans, Ukrainians, Scandinavians and, in a province that has not been sympathetic to Quebec's campaign for autonomy, a fair-sized and happy French-speaking community, mostly north of Edmonton.

With its soaring skyscrapers, Alberta's second-largest city (population 710,000) has come a long way from its frontier days as

Carrying the flag for Canada in Calgary's dynamic downtown.

a fort where the North West Mounted Police tried to control unruly whisky peddlers. But the basic boisterousness remains. Though oil was discovered in the nearby Turner Valley in 1914, until the oil boom of the 1970s, Calgary remained just a bouncing cow-town, but a cow-town nonetheless. The Calgary Stampede rodeo show was its greatest claim to fame—and for many still is. The difference is that the new breed of bankers and businessmen now half-conceal their cowboy boots beneath a stylishly cut Giorgio Armani suit.

For visitors, Calgary serves principally as a gateway to the Badlands, dinosaur country and the Rockies. As constant modernization has removed almost all its older buildings, the town itself can easily be visited in one or two days. The region's history is beautifully displayed in the Glenbow Museum—one of the best in North America—and you'll find something of the town's past in a reconstruction of Fort Calgary.

Downtown

The city centre is tall but quite small and easy to get around on foot, with a tram system running up and down for free and charging only a small fare for trips to the outskirts. Designed for brutal winter days when the mellowing Chinook wind is not operative, a network of covered walkways known as the Plus 15 Walking System—$4^1/2$ m (15 ft) above ground level, except for the subterranean galleries—links office buildings and shops through much of the downtown area. Unfortunately, despite strategically located maps, the numerous shopping malls turn the network into a maze that only seasoned locals can figure out. Try walking on the street.

CHINOOK

The air is dry and clear in southern Alberta, with more sun and less rain than over in BC. The winds blowing in from the Pacific Ocean lose their moisture by condensation on the western slopes of the Rockies. In winter, after the wind clears the mountain barrier, it brings to the Alberta plains a warm, dry air mass that may melt the snow and cause temperature increases of up to 22°C (40°F) within a few hours. This phenomenon is called a Chinook—similar to what Europe's Alpine countries know as the *Föhn*, though with nothing like the same dramatic effect. Originally it was a name given by Oregon settlers to a moist Pacific wind blowing from the direction of a Chinook Indian camp.

Walking tall among the towers: the Family of Man.

Glenbow Museum

The beauty of this unique museum, located at 130 Ninth Avenue SE, is in the way visitors from all over the world can relate life in Western Canada, from its beginnings to the present day, to their own personal experience. In an attractive modern setting on four superbly lit floors, whether it be ceremonial costumes, kitchen implements, jewellery or cosmetics, the emphasis is always on intercultural comparisons. In one hall, the weapons and armour of a Japanese samurai are shown together with those of a Cree Indian, a medieval European Crusader and a Canadian infantryman in World War II. The art and artefacts of Canada's Native Peoples can constantly be compared with their equivalents among European settlers. The artful simplicity of Indians' washing implements is set against the drudgery of the immigrants' scrubbing-boards and hand-operated laundry wringers.

In the Blackfoot Sikika Indians' monumental *tipi* we see its cleverly separated sleeping areas and how the tent-flaps let the smoke out but not back in, kept out the wind and rain or brought in summer breezes. Again, this opulent dwelling can be compared to the Canadian pioneers'

72

spartan log cabin. Western Canada's story is also traced from the primitive implements of the earliest fur trappers or gold and coal miners to the tools and machinery of the railway-builders and modern oil-drillers. Among the most touching exhibits are the clothes made in the 1930s Depression from ingeniously recycled flour bags, with sleeves from old socks and "bejewelled" with chains of safety pins. In the exhibit of prized possessions brought from the Old Country is a carpenter's intricately hand-made toolbox demonstrating in its making better than any letter of recommendation all his skills with inlaid woods. There is also a good collection of Canadian paintings from the pioneering days to the modern era.

Calgary Tower

Every town must have one. At 101 Ninth Avenue SW, the observation deck on this landmark tower is 190 m (623 ft) high, looking out over the city to the Rocky Mountains. Immediately below it is a revolving restaurant for you to enjoy the same view over an expensive steak.

Fort Calgary

At 750 Ninth Avenue, where the Bow River is joined by the appropriately named Elbow River, this is a reconstruction of the North West Mounties' wooden fort that began the city. It is being painstakingly carried out with building materials and tools like those used for the 1875 original. Also on show is a CPR worker's log cabin and hospital. Should you want to, you can be photographed in the full scarlet regalia of a Mountie's uniform. Nearby are the town's two oldest surviving buildings, the Fort superintendent's Deane House (1906), and the Hudson's Bay Company's Hunt House.

Prince's Island

A footbridge takes you over to this pleasant park in the middle of

---

ALBERTA HIGHLIGHTS

– **Glenbow Museum**: exquisitely presented view of Western Canadian life (p. 72).
– **Head-Smashed-In Buffalo Jump**: splendid setting for ancient Blackfoot Indian buffalo hunt (p. 75).
– **Royal Tyrrell Museum**: introduction to age of dinosaurs (p. 77).
– **West Edmonton Mall**: mind-boggling shoppers' paradise (p. 81).

In July Calgary goes wilder than the Wild West ever was.

the Bow River, with picnic areas and a good restaurant. But don't even think of taking a dip in the river's icy waters with lethal undercurrents.

Calgary Stampede

Is it more difficult to milk a wild cow than to ride a bull? Wrestle a steer or "break" a bronco? Find out during ten days every July at the Calgary Stampede, held out at Stampede Park. Those are only a few of the crazy things they've been doing here since 1912. They called it then the Greatest Outdoor Show in the World and have seen no reason to change the claim now.

The great event also includes livestock shows and auctions, garden shows and displays of Indian dancing and craftware, a high-stakes casino and all the fun of a country fair. The show begins with an astounding parade of baton-twirling majorettes, cowboys, Blackfoot Indians in ceremonial costume, prize cattle, the Mayor of Calgary and any other local dignitaries running for re-election. Then the very serious rodeo begins, $500,000 in prize money for all that calf-roping, Indian buffalo riding and steer-wrestling, with the daily climax being the lunatic chuckwagon races for the Rangeland Derby.

Life and limb are risked in nine races every evening as four-horse wagons like those that brought food to the cowboys during the prairie roundup hurtle around the stadium at breakneck speed. Barbecue beef dinners are washed down with plenty of beer and whisky and the next day begins bright and early with open-air breakfasts of bacon, pancakes and flapjacks. Yahoo!

Head-Smashed-in Buffalo Jump

Some 175 km (109 miles) due south of Calgary off Highway 2 is one of Canada's great natural monuments. In an evocative prairie setting of rolling grassland stretching from the abrupt sandstone cliff of a higher plateau is the ancient Indian buffalo hunting ground, now designed a UNESCO World Heritage Site. Going back to at least 3600 BC, hunters in late summer used to drive herds of buffalo over the cliff to their deaths to provide a huge store of meat, hide, bone and horn; almost everything the tribe needed for food, clothing and tools to see them through the upcoming winter.

A harmoniously designed Interpretive Centre has been built into the cliff to illustrate the Plains Indians' buffalo hunting culture from ancient times to its end after Contact with the Euro-

WHOSE HEAD WAS SMASHED IN?

As the story goes, a young Blackfoot brave 150 years ago sheltered beneath a cliff ledge to watch the death jump of hundreds of buffalo. The first beasts plunged past him, but gradually they piled up all around, trapping him in his hideout. His people found him with his skull crushed by the carcasses.

peans. An observation platform on top of the cliff looks west to the Olsen Creek Basin where the buffalo herd was gathered and gradually lured and driven towards the cliff. From the basin, two rows of stone cairns can be seen extending 8 km (5 miles) in a narrowing "drive lane" that forced the buffaloes over the cliff-jump. Immediately below the cliff to the east is the "kill site", an exposed escarpment 100 m long and 10 m high—it was once 10 m higher but the land has been filled in by the grassed-over debris and bones from thousands of years of hunting. On the flat prairie, beyond the slope is the Blackfoot campsite where the buffalo was butchered and processed. You can walk along well-marked paths around the kill site and camping area.

THE BADLANDS
Drumheller, Edmonton

The severely eroded, hopelessly arid Badlands east of Calgary were so named by hunters, prospective pioneer farmers and fur traders looking for food and shelter. But for the adventurous modern traveller, and especially geologists and palaeontologists, the lunar landscapes extending on either side of Red Deer River Valley are a genuinely unforgettable sight. The canyons and weird hoodoos—rock mushroom pillars of buff or grey sandstone streaked with purple ironstone—look unchanged in millions of years, as if the dinosaurs dropped dead just yesterday.

Drumheller

Some 130 km (80 miles) northeast of Calgary, the old coal-mining town serves as a centre from which to tour the land of the dinosaurs and prehistoric fossils. Along Highway 9, you will pass the wheat farms of Hutterite communities, originally from Slovakia. The women of this austere religious sect wear dirndl dresses with apron and headscarf while the men are all in black with wide-brimmed hats and long beards. Just southwest of Drumheller, turn off to the signposted Horseshoe Canyon viewpoint for a first sight of classical Badland.

Royal Tyrrell Museum of Palaeontology

A short drive northwest of town, this superlative museum is an absolute must as an introduction to the Dinosaur Trail and Dinosaur Provincial Park. Even the most jaded combatant of Jurassic Park dinomania will be stimulated by the lucidly presented exhibits, at once serious and entertaining without a trace of commercial hype. Skeletons of gigantic and comparatively miniature but always lifesize prehistoric creatures, amphibians, birds, reptiles and mammals are set in superbly conceived natural habitats. Tyrannosaurus Rex is there, 14 m (45 ft) long and 6 m (19 ft) tall, and Albertosaurus, too, but also the amazing Dimetrodon reptile with a great, as yet unexplained spiny "sail" on its back. And the sweet little duck-billed Lambeosaurus, with her baby. The terrifying skeleton of a sabre-toothed tiger, neatly named Smilodon, is enthusiastically poised to attack a Plains Bison. Next to Dinosaur Hall, take time out to visit one of the museum's most

Sizing up a mammoth in the Tyrrell Museum.

attractive exhibits, the light and airy Palaeoconservatory greenhouse for over 100 living descendants of plants that grew 350 to 15 million years ago. They have been brought here not only from the southern United States but as far away as Malaysia, Singapore, Australia and New Zealand.

Dinosaur Trail

Continue northwest from the museum on Highway 838 on a circuit of 48 km (30 miles) around the Red Deer River Valley and otherwise barren natural habitat of the prehistoric creatures you have just seen. On the way, stop off at the signposted viewpoint on Horsethief Canyon, the perfect hideout for rustlers.

TYRRELL'S TREASURE

In 1884, Joseph Tyrrell, a young geologist employed by the government to find coal, came across the fossilized bones of the Albertosaurus sarcophagus, a 65-million-year-old Alberta carcass eater. Found on a hillside above the Red Deer River, the fossils were sent back to Ottawa for analysis. It took another 30 years before Canada joined the great dinosaur hunt that has thus far uncovered remains of more than 90 dinosaurs and 100 other prehistoric creatures in Alberta's Badlands.

Southeast of Drumheller you can clamber around a group of hoodoos. Further east is the disused Atlas Coal Mine to remind us what started the dinosaur craze.

Dinosaur Provincial Park

True dinosaur enthusiasts make the 175 km (109 miles) drive from Drumheller and are rewarded with the most spectacular landscapes in all the Alberta Badlands. This World Heritage Site protects a seemingly inexhaustible source of fossils. The ongoing dig is out-of-bounds to private motorists, but some unearthed skeletons have been left in place and can be seen on a guided Badlands Bus Tour organized from the field station.

Edmonton

The citizens of the provincial capital hate to admit it, but it remains true that foreign visitors who do come here head straight for that West Edmonton Shopping Mall—or fly in and drive right out again to the Rockies through Jasper National Park. The town (population 750,000) is attractive enough for Albertans, with more galleries, arts festivals and a usually better ice hockey team than its great rival, Calgary. Edmonton's share of the oil wealth has also built an imposing modern downtown area, but most people find it pleasanter to hang

out among the open-air cafés, restaurants, galleries, bookshops and boutiques of the Old Strathcona neighbourhood south of the North Saskatchewan River.

Edmonton Art Gallery

On Sir Winston Churchill Square, the municipal gallery can claim the best collection of Canadian painting in Alberta, including good examples of Ontario's much admired Tom Thomson and the Group of Seven as well as BC's Emily Carr and leading painters of the prairie provinces.

West Edmonton Mall

This shoppers' Valhalla is located on 87th Avenue between 170th and 178th streets. Among the 11 mentions it rates in the *Guinness Book of World Records* are, of course, the "largest shopping mall in the world", 49 ha (110 acres), but also the "world's largest car park", for 20,000 vehicles. The rest is numbers. West Edmonton Mall joke: "How many customers does it take to pay for the Mall's 325,000 light fixtures?" Answer: 140,000 customers a day raiding over 800 shops, including 19 cinemas, 110 restaurants or fast food outlets, 13 nightclubs, 10 major department stores, skating rink, water park with four submarines (more, it says rather unpatriotically, than the Canadian Navy), four dolphins playing in the indoor lagoon, 2-m-high waves for surfing, 22 waterslides, 20 aquariums and a bird sanctuary (only one).

FUR, GOLD AND OIL

Edmonton's history is a tale of four dates. In 1795, Hudson's Bay Company set up a fort here for its fur traders. They used the services of Cree, Assiniboine and Blackfoot Indians, an act of rare diplomacy inasmuch as these tribes were usually at war with each other. In 1897, the Klondyke gold rush brought men pouring into Edmonton, misled by local newspapers into thinking there was a safe route from this supply centre to the Yukon. Of the 1,600 prospectors who came, none made it in time to find any gold, many perished on the way and others, hearing the bad news, never bothered to leave town. The city, at least, prospered from the mini-boom enough to stake a successful claim in 1905 as capital of the new province, over the competing bids of Banff and Calgary. Finally, in 1947, the discovery of petroleum in nearby Leduc launched Edmonton's career as an oil town, with 10,000 wells surrounding it by the 1960s. The local ice hockey team is understandably known as the Edmonton Oilers.

The hallowed monuments of the seemingly endless prairies are the mighty grain elevators that rise like fortresses out of the fields of wheat, barley, oats and rye. Saskatchewan prides itself on being known as "Canada's bread basket," but Manitoba can make an equal claim, setting a world-wide standard for bread wheat with the highgrade grain grown in its southwestern Souris plains. While Saskatchewan's population is still overwhelmingly of British stock, Manitoba adds a rich ethnic mix from Eastern and Southern Europe.

Get at least a feel for the Prairie Provinces with a visit to the two provincial capitals.

Regina, Saskatchewan

It is second in population (180,000) to Saskatoon, but has made enormous progress since the first settlers arrived in 1880. They found the banks of Wascana Creek heaped high with buffalo bones left by Indian hunters. So Pile o'Bones was the town's first name until it changed to its present more majestic title paying homage to Victoria. The creek has been dammed to form a lake in Wascana Centre Park, which offers a rare chance to see trees in southern Saskatchewan.

Diefenbaker Homestead

Saskatchewan's most illustrious son, their first federal prime minister, was a feisty Conservative popularly known as Dief the Chief. His tiny wooden home in Borden was moved to Wascana Centre Park as a historic shrine to demonstrate the simple life led by the province's beloved country boy before he set off for fame and glory in Ottawa.

Royal Canadian Mounted Police Barracks

Headquarters for the Mounties until 1920, it has kept the crime detection laboratory and training centre here (west of downtown along 11th Avenue to Sleigh Square). The museum tells of the Mounties' adventures with Plains Indians, gold prospectors and American whiskey peddlers. Visit the old mess hall, known as the Little Chapel on the Square, with its bizarre stained-glass portraits of Mounties where you would normally expect saints.

Government House

West of downtown at 4607 Dewdney Avenue, this was the lieutenant governor's late 19th-century yellow-brick residence. It has been charmingly restored with original furnishings to show

how the politicians of old lived in considerably more style than Dief the Chief. At weekends, English-style high tea is served in the ballroom.

Winnipeg, Manitoba

Built where the Assiniboine and Red rivers meet at the confluence known locally as The Forks, the town lies plumb in the geographical centre of Canada. This makes it the major distribution point for the country's agricultural products. Its 620,000 residents account for nearly two-thirds of Manitoba's total population and include solid communities of Ukrainian, German, Polish, Jewish, Dutch, Hungarian and Italian origin. Every August, many of them come out in force for the Folklorama festival to present the music, dance and above all cuisine of their ancestors.

Visitors from October to May can enjoy performances of the Winnipeg Symphony Orchestra and the town's opera and ballet companies in the Centennial Centre.

The Forks

The sprawling railway yards behind the Union Station have been transformed into a lively entertainment district with shops, galleries, delicatessens, ice-cream parlours, restaurants and an outdoor amphitheatre. Plaques along the river bank describe the exploits of pioneers at the spot where enterprising fur trader Pierre Gaultier de la Vérendrye founded in 1737 Fort Rouge, the precursor of Winnipeg.

Museum of Man and Nature

At 190 Rupert Avenue, this excellent museum combines the region's story since prehistoric times with a vivid presentation of Canadian fauna set in their natural habitats: polar bears in the Arctic tundra, wolves in the forest and mountain, even repulsive insects in the wilds of Manitoba, all with lifelike sound-effects. Manitoba's ethnic groups appear in their homesteads in traditional costume, along with a meticulous reconstruction of a Winnipeg street in the 1920s. The star attraction is the reconstructed vessel, the *Nonsuch* ketch which in 1668 started the Hudson's Bay Company on its way to fortune in the fur trade.

Winnipeg Art Gallery

At 300 Memorial Boulevard, this thoroughly modern, wedge-shaped museum has a good permanent collection of 20th-century Canadian and American artists, shown in rotation, but it is above all renowned for its broad range of Inuit Eskimo sculpture, unrivalled in North America.

83

NATURE NOTES

Bear. In the national parks area, there are perhaps 200 grizzly *Ursus arctos horribilis*, distinguished by their grey-streaked dark brown fur. On all fours, father bear is just 1.20 m (4 ft) high, but when he rears up on his hindlegs he can measure up to 2.5 m (8 ft) tall. He reaches his fighting weight of 360 kg (800 lb) on a dinner of deer or elk, but won't turn up his snout at an entrée of ants or other insects and a side portion of plants, roots and berries. He doesn't particularly like, but will occasionally eat, a piece of *Homo sapiens*, so keep out of his way. If you do meet up with one, your best chance of survival is just to curl up slowly on the ground, play dead and he may believe you and go away. Bad news: the black bear (*Ursus americanus*) is smaller but not more friendly and doesn't buy that playing-dead stuff. Just retreat to your vehicle as discreetly as you can.

Beavers. After near extinction, this national symbol of diligence is back in force in the Rockies, especially in late summer. They are often spotted near Yoho's Emerald Lake scampering around, damming up a stream with mud, sticks and gravel to form their own little pond so they can swim safely to where their favourite food is in the upcoming winter. This waterway is an escape route from the creatures for whom they are in turn richly nourishing—predator coyotes, lynx and wolverines. The beaver's distinctive large flat tail acts as a rudder to steer it through the water.

Dinosaur Timetable. To get a perspective on Alberta's pre-historic fossils, remember that the first dinosaurs appeared on earth along with the first mammal in the Triassic period about 200 million years ago. Giant dinosaurs thrived in the Jurassic period between 190 and 135 million years ago. They died out 65 million years before our era.

Fish-Watching. With the national parks phasing out the use of bait and lead weights for fishing in their lakes and rivers, the new sport for "reformed" anglers, on a par with bird-watching, has become fish-watching at spawning time. In

May, rainbow trout spawn right under Yoho's Emerald Lake bridge. At O'Hara Lake, they do their thing in June and can be seen from the shoreline near the lake's outlet. Brook trout are more shy and go to the far end of Emerald Lake to spawn in October, more easily seen from a canoe than at the water's edge.

Lumber. To defenders of the Canadian forest, modern technology has proved at once a curse and a blessing. In the old days, "cut and run" lumberjacks axed everything in sight, razing whole forests. The advent of power-saws and bulldozers at first proved even more devastating than the axe. Now, say the lumber companies, forestry scientists have moved in to cull trees more selectively by computer-programmed surveys. But the computer also enables the logging to go faster…

Salmon. The Pacific salmon you are most likely to be served in a Canadian restaurant is the sockeye, appetizingly red and just rich enough in oils to maintain its succulence when grilled or poached. The four other species of Canadian salmon are pink, coho, chum and chinook. Commercial fisheries like the sockeye because it keeps its colour and flavour after processing for canning. The pink is nice, but small, and the chum or dog is less oily and so easier to smoke, stocked by the Indians for the winter. Sportsmen go for the coho, a champion high-jumper, and the chinook —"king" to Americans—for its feisty fighting habits. Both may weigh in over 11 kg (25 lb), with chinook sometimes coming in at 18 kg (40 lb).

Whales. Whale-lovers come from all over the world to BC, especially Vancouver Island's Pacific Rim National Park to watch for a rare killer whale (orca), found in resident pods around the southern end of the island. More common are the migrating grey whales, blueish-grey without a dorsal fin, about 14 m (45 ft) long and weighing up to 50 tons. Each spring, these great mammals pass through on their 8,000-km (5,000-mile) northbound migration from breeding lagoons in Baja, Mexico, up to summer feeding grounds in the Bering Straits off the coast of Siberia. 85

Shopping

These days, world commerce being what it is, you can buy practically everything everywhere. Prices may vary, but there is very little that is totally unique. What is special is Western Canada's great outdoors life. You're bound to find the appropriate items to go with it, either to enjoy it better while you're here or to recapture the experience back home.

Where?

The enterprise of the fur traders who opened up the West has been channelled into first-class chains of department stores. The most famous of course remains the Hudson's Bay Company, but Eaton's is a worthy rival. There are branches in every city's downtown area as well as the malls—Vancouver's Pacific Plaza, Calgary's Stephen Avenue and Toronto Dominion Square and above all the fabled West Edmonton Mall. Other great shopping areas are Vancouver's Robson Street, Granville Island and Chinatown, more offbeat in Calgary's revitalized Kensington neighbourhood.

The top museums' shops are the best places to look for arts and crafts—Museum of Anthropology in Vancouver, the Glenbow in Calgary, Royal Tyrrell at Drumheller and for Inuit work, the Winnipeg Art Museum.

Away from the big cities, village grocery stores advertise great country auctions for old-fashioned antiques—and fascinating junk. If you're looking for a fossil, you'll probably be able to buy one in Drumheller.

What?

You will find top-quality sporting equipment and all-weather clothing designed for the region's backwoods. The native peoples' arts and crafts have recaptured their traditional high quality with the new pride in their ethnic identity.

Clothes

The bonus for the west coast's, let's say, *trying* weather is in the superlative parkas, rugged hunting-jackets, fishermen's leggings. The brightly coloured chequered

Wherever you go, the streets are designed to make shopping a pleasure.

shirts are no longer considered corny, they're warm, comfortable and *authentic*. In Calgary, the cowboy boots, leather belts and hats are superb but by no means cheap.

The Northwest Coast Indians' practically stormproof Cowichan heavy-knit woollen sweaters are beautifully made, embroidered with whale, thunderbird or other totemic motifs, and they often come with matching gloves and bonnets. For footwear, try a pair of soft Inuit fur and sealskin mukluks or feather-light Indian moccasins.

Craftware

At the museum shops, look for Indian carvings in wood or black argillite, basketry, silver jewellery and fine beadwork. Inuit artists work in steatite soapstone, onyx, bone and scrimshaw (etched ivory), with a good selection in the Inuit gallery in Vancouver's Gastown.

Jewellery

BC jade is fashioned into fine earrings, pendants, necklaces and bracelets and sold in Vancouver's Chinatown and in the Rocky Mountain resort hotel boutiques, where you will also find surprisingly delicate rings made from the local granite.

Electronics

Laptops and other computer equipment are much cheaper than in Europe, but check on compatibility with electric power requirements and after-sales service warranties overseas before purchasing.

Music

CDs are a real bargain, with discount stores offering great year-round "special sales". For videocassettes, again, you'd be well advised to check on compatibility for European equipment.

Gourmet Foods

Three Canadian delicacies to take home as souvenirs: a whole smoked salmon, which delicatessen shops sell specially packaged for travellers, a good bottle of maple syrup for grandma and Canadian rye whisky for grandad, or vice versa.

Dining Out

Nobody ever pretended Western Canada was a gourmet paradise, but there is no denying the quality of its seafood from the Pacific, its freshwater fish and the beef of Alberta. And as a change, the cosmopolitan cities offer fine Chinese, Japanese, or Italian and other European restaurants. Good French establishments are harder to find, but BC wines now make excellent alternatives to Bordeaux and Burgundy.

Fish

Freshly caught Pacific salmon, sockeye or chinook, is at its best when served baked or grilled without frills, at most with a few sliced almonds. Shrimp and crab, but also halibut, bass and trout are exceptional. In Vancouver's many Japanese restaurants the freshness of the local seafood make the sashimi and sushi the best outside Osaka and Kyoto.

Meat

Top choice goes to Alberta's prime rib of beef and sirloin steaks as big and succulent as anything Texas can produce. You may prefer to go for roast lamb, from the flocks reared on the BC Gulf Islands' Saltspring.

Vegetables and Fruit

Okanagan Valley provides superb green vegetables and plums, peaches, apricots, strawberries and cherries to satisfy the most delicate palate. Or eat an apple together with the tangy Armstrong cheddar cheese.

Drinks

Beer remains the national drink, but the red and white wines from BC's Okanagan Valley are fast taking over. Try a fruity red Cabernet Sauvignon or full-bodied Merlot, or perhaps a light white Riesling or more fragrant Gewürztraminer. Quails' Gate, Mission Hill, Calon and Gray Monk are among the better labels to look for. And Canada's rye whisky is drunk by connoisseurs as a *digestif*, always neat and without ice.

A word about the coffee: after years of "instant", Western Canada, with the rest of North America, has suddenly gone crazy for Italian coffee: espresso, cappuccino, milky caffelatte or diluted americano, all expensive, but far better than before.

Sports

Water Sports

You'll find swimming at its most pleasant in the Pacific, on the beaches of Vancouver and Vancouver Island, best of all the Pacific Rim National Park's fine sandy Long Beach. Surfers come here, too, for the spectacular waves. Only the hardiest do not find the lakes and rivers too cool, but even then they should watch out for dangerous undercurrents. Windsurfing is a better bet, exhilarating on Rocky Mountain lakes such as Maligne Lake in Jasper's park or the Emerald Lake in Yoho NP.

The fast-flowing Fraser and Thompson rivers invite the adventurous to try variations on whitewater rafting in canoes and kayaks—the sport's "capital" being Lytton, at the confluence.

Fishing

Despite growing environmentalist opposition, deep-sea fishing for salmon and halibut is still an active sport on the Pacific coast. Rocky Mountain lakes and rivers are rich in pike, whitefish, freshwater bass, trout and char—but remember you must get a permit from the local park wardens, be prepared to fish without bait or lead weights and observe maximum catch and possession limits of only two game fish on any one day.

Tennis and Golf

Excellent facilities for both sports are available in and around Vancouver, Victoria and Calgary, but especially up at the Whistler resort in summer and also in the Okanagan Valley. Hotels can arrange for private clubs to admit guest members.

Horseback Riding

This is a major activity on Vancouver Island in Pacific Rim National Park, at the resort hotels in Banff and Jasper and in the cowboy country around Calgary.

Skiing

This has become a popular all-season sport at the Whistler resort with slopes open well into the summer on both Blackcomb and Whistler mountains. Elsewhere, especially in the Rockies, spring and late autumn visitors will have no trouble finding cross-country skiing as a fast way of getting around the mountains.

And you can always do it by bicycle...

The Hard Facts

To plan your trip, here are some of the practical details you should know about Western Canada:

Airports

Most international flights serve Vancouver, Calgary, Edmonton and Winnipeg. The terminals all provide banking, car-hire and tourist information office services, in addition to duty-free shop, restaurant and snack bar facilities. If you don't have transport arranged, taxi and bus services are available to take you downtown. From Calgary, coach services go directly to Banff and Lake Louise, and from Edmonton directly to Jasper National Park.

Climate

Temperatures at Western Canada's lower altitudes reach a pleasant 24°C (75°F) in summer. In BC, the weather around Vancouver and Victoria and along the southwestern Pacific coast is much milder than in the interior, apart from the exceptionally warm Okanagan Valley. The Rockies are cooler, though pleasantly warm in high summer. Calgary and southern Alberta enjoy the region's most sunny climate, with that special asset of the Chinook to warm up winter days.

Communications

The Canadian Post Office seems to be no more efficient than any other government-run operation around the world. If you have urgent mail, ask your hotel about the international courier services available. Fax and telephone are the easiest ways to communicate. Telephone cards enable you to avoid hotel surcharges, but they do not operate on quite the same magnetic basis as in Europe, requiring a system of individual code numbering as a prefix to the number you want to dial. Ask your hotel receptionist to explain the intricacies.

Crime

Canada's big cities are generally a lot safer than those across the border. Pickpockets, however, do work the tourist beaches, campsites and mountain resorts. You will avoid trouble with elementary precautions. Leave your valuables in the hotel safe and keep your belongings out of sight when parking your car.

As a wise precaution, make photocopies of your passport, driver's license and credit cards and keep them separate from the originals.

Driving

If renting a car, be sure to have a valid national licence or International Driving Permit. Payment is almost always by credit card only. Check on the exact extent of varying insurance coverages, personal, fire, collision, theft, etc. Roads, except in the remotest mountain areas, are excellent. As in the US, drive on the right, overtake on the left, but you'll find distances and speed limits in kilometres, not miles. Maximum speed on highways and expressways is 100 kph (60 mph), in town 50 kph (30 mph) and in signposted children's areas 30 kph (20 mph). The use of seatbelts is compulsory, front and rear. Fuel is sold by the litre, always unleaded unless you specify otherwise.

Electric Current

As in the US, 110 volts, 60 cycles AC, with US-style flat-pin plugs. Bring an adaptor for your European appliances, local hotels rarely have them.

Emergencies

Most problems can be handled at your hotel desk. In big cities, the telephone number for police, fire or ambulance service is **911**, else-where dial 0 for operator. Consular help is there only for critical situations, lost passports or worse, *not* for lost cash or plane tickets.

Essentials

Travel light, especially as far as clothing is concerned. Canadians will probably be dressed more casually than you, so you won't need much formal wear. Pack a sun-hat and add a sweater for cool evenings. Good walking shoes are vital, especially for the mountains, and easy-to-kick-off sandals or moccasins for the beach. Bring along sun-block, insect-repellent and a pocket torch (flashlight).

Formalities

A valid passport is all that most of you will need—for US citizens, just an identity card (but *not* a driver's licence). You may be asked on entry to show your return ticket. No special health certificates are required for European or American citizens.

Health

Most health problems are from too much sun. Avoid excessive direct exposure to the summer sun. Wear a hat, use a sun-screen, and keep to the shady side of the street when sightseeing. Insect bites from mosquitoes and black flies can be a bother in summer, 93 so bring plenty of insect-repellent. Hospital care is first-rate, but medical fees can be expensive if you do not have health insurance to cover your stay in Canada. Check before leaving home. If you anticipate need of prescription medicines, take your own as you may not find the exact equivalent on the spot.

Language

English is of course the local language, for many indistinguishable from the American variety, except for little variations like *aboat* for *about* and the giveaway *eh?* tagged onto the end of every other sentence.

With the exception of some tour guides, western Canadians speak very little French or any other foreign language for that matter.

Media

The closest thing Canada has to a national newspaper is the very good Toronto *Globe and Mail*. Otherwise, local papers stick almost exclusively to local news. In the sea of FM popular music and talk-show stations, CBC (Canadian Broadcasting Corporation) radio stands out for its news, cultural and public affairs programming. Most large hotels have TV cable and satellite facilities to receive both US and Canadian stations, with possible

access to BBC, French, German, Spanish and Italian programmes, too.

Money

The Canadian dollar is the poor sister of the American, but comes in similar denominations: coins: 1¢ (penny), 5¢ (nickel), 10¢ (dime), 25¢ (quarter), $1 (loonie), $2; notes (bills): $5, $10, $20, $50, $100, $1000. Almost all international credit cards are accepted. You will often have to go to a currency exchange rather than a bank to change foreign currency other than US dollars.

Opening Hours

Banks generally open 10 a.m. to 3 p.m. (many later on Thursday and Friday).

Shops are open 10 a.m. to 6 p.m. (many later Thursday and Friday); Saturday 10 a.m. to 5 p.m., some open Sunday afternoon 12 to 5 p.m. A few convenience stores, mini-supermarkets, operate 24 hours a day.

Main Post Offices usually open 9 a.m. to 5 p.m. Monday to Friday, with minor outlets open much later in convenience stores.

Museums are usually closed Monday, otherwise, as a very general indication, open 10 a.m. to 5 or 6 p.m. Tuesday to Saturday, and often Sunday, too, but check with the local tourist information office.

Photography
Every imaginable form of film, colour, black and white, video is available, with super-fast development services. Most museums allow cameras, but sometimes for an extra fee, with restrictions on the use of flash.

Public Holidays
When a holiday falls on a Sunday, the following day is often observed as a holiday. In Western Canada, offices and businesses are closed on the following official holidays:

January 1	New Year's Day
moveable	Good Friday
	Easter Monday
mid-May	Victoria Day
July 1	Canada Day
1st Mon in Aug. (except Yukon)	Civic Holiday
3rd Mon in Aug. (Yukon)	Discovery Day
1st Mon in Sep.	Labor Day
2nd Mon in Oct.	Thanksgiving
November 11	Remembrance Day
December 25	Christmas Day

Public Transport
For Vancouver, BC Transit operates an efficiently integrated network of services by bus, light-rail (the driverless SkyTrain) and ferry (SeaBus), with tickets valid on all three. Calgary and Edmonton Transit operate similarly integrated services of bus and light-train or tram. Between cities, Greyhound coaches operate right across Canada, while VIA Rail has taken over most of the CPR and CNR passenger network.

Time Difference
Western Canada covers three time zones:

British Columbia:
Pacific Standard Time GMT –8

Alberta and W. Saskatchewan:
Mountain ST   GMT –7

E. Saskatchewan and Manitoba:
Central ST   GMT –6

All provinces except East Saskatchewan put the clocks forward an hour from the first Sunday in April to the last Sunday in October, for Daylight Saving Time.

Tipping
The general rule is 10 to 15% for waiters, taxi-drivers, hairdressers and tour guides and $1–2 per day for hotel maids.

Toilets
Usually impeccable and in every public establishment, known as rest rooms, bathrooms, washrooms, sometimes even toilets. At service stations, you may need to ask for a key.

INDEX

Athabasca Falls 65

Banff 59–60

Banff NP 59–63

Botanical Beach 40–42

Bow Valley Parkway 62

Britannia Beach 32

Broken Group Islands 44

Calgary 69–74

Cathedral Grove 42

Columbia Icefield 65

Craigellachie 54

Crowfoot Glacier 63

Dinosaur Provincial Park 79

Dinosaur Trail 79

Drumheller 76–79

Edmonton 79–80

Emerald Lake 56

Fraser Canyon 47

Galiano Island 45

Garibaldi Provincial Park 33

Glacier NP 55

Grouse Mountain 27

Gulf Islands 45

Head-Smashed-in Buffalo Jump 75

Hell's Gate 48

Hope 47

Icefields Parkway 63

Inside Passage 45

Jasper 66

Jasper National Park 65–67

Kamloops 49

Kelowna 51

Kicking Horse Pass 57

Kootenay NP 57–58

Kootenay Valley Viewpoint 58

Lake Louise 62

Little Qualicum Falls 42

Long Beach 44

Lytton 49–50

Maligne Canyon 66

Maligne Lake 67

Maligne Valley 66

Marble Canyon 58

Medicine Lake 67

Minnewanka Loop 60–62

Mistaya Canyon 63

Moraine Lake 62–63

Mount Wardle 58

Mt Revelstoke 54–55

Mt Revelstoke NP 53–55

O'Hara Lake 57

Okanagan Valley 50–51

Olive Lake 58

Osoyoos 51

Pacific Rim National Park 44–45

Paint Pots 58

Parker's Ridge 65

Penticton 51

Peyto Lake 63

Port Alberni 42

Regina 82

Revelstoke 54

Rogers Pass 55

Saltspring Island 45

Saskatchewan River Crossing 63–65

Sea to Sky Highway 31–32

Shannon Falls 32

Sinclair Canyon 58

Sooke 40

Squamish 32–33

Squilax 50

Sunwapta Falls 65

Takakkaw Falls 57

Thompson Canyon 47

Tofino 44

Vancouver 19–31
  Beaches 28–29, 30
  Chinatown 27
  Downtown 21–26
  Gastown 25–26
  Museums 29–31
  Yaletown 25

Vermilion Pass 58

Victoria 35–40

Wapta Falls 55–56

West Coast Trail 44–45

Whistler 33

Winnipeg 83

Yale 47–48

Yoho NP 55–57

Seattle

Emerald City

Bright and energetic, Seattle is blessed with one of those natural locations that render public relations superfluous. Its bay on Puget Sound is surrounded by the green, green country of Washington state with the snowcapped Olympic and Cascade mountains looming in the background, and Mount Rainier towering over them all. The climate is fresh and moist enough to earn the town its by-line of the "Emerald City".

In town, Pioneer Square, dating from the 19th century, and traditional waterside markets are overshadowed by contemporary architecture. The Seattle Center, with its distinctive Space Needle, offers magnificent views of the city and surrounding scenery. On a clear day, it is possible to see Mount St Helen's about 265 km (165 miles) south of the city.

Few traces remain of the Seattle's colourful, if rough, beginnings in the 1850s. The superb natural outer harbour, Elliot Bay, was ideal for the transport of timber brought down from the vast forests of the Northwest, as well as the import of luxuries from the Orient. Seattle was also a springboard for the Alaska and Klondike gold rushes of the 1880s and 1890s. Although the timber industry still thrives in Seattle, the town's present-day prosperity is linked more strongly with that of the aeronautical industry and computer software.

The region holds many attractions: the nearby mountains offer top-class skiing, climbing and hiking, and relaxation is all too easy in and around the countless lakes dotted with boats ranging in size from tiny dinghies to majestic yachts.

A Brief History

19th century

The first settlement is established on the western shore of Elliot Bay at Alki Point in 1815. Two years later, the expanding sawmill town is planned and laid out, named Seattle after the friendly Indian chief Seathl. Successive disasters—an Indian raid in 1856, anti-Chinese riots in the 1880s, the fire of 1889—hinder development until the railroad arrives in 1893. Seattle takes advantage of the Alaskan gold rush and growing trade with the Far East to forge its own prosperity.

20th century

Expansion continues, but at a slower pace. The Panama Canal (1914) encourages more shipping to the US East Coast and Europe. The Lake Washington Canal, built in

1916, creates a route from inner to out... fortunes are hard hit by the Great Depression of ... 30s. The switch to a wartime economy mobilizes natural resources and industrial capacity. Shipyards serve the war in the Pacific, and the new aircraft industry gains a foothold. Business slumps again during the 1950s.

Seattle draws the world's attention to its progress and potential by holding an International World's Fair in 1962. The city is now a major centre on the Pacific coast for forestry and air- and spacecraft, for the financial world, and for futuristic electronics and biomedical industries.

Sightseeing

The attractions of cosmopolitan Seattle are immensely varied, catering to every taste, whether for art and music, sightseeing, shopping or dining out at one of many fine restaurants, or simply sipping a coffee in one of the hundreds of coffee houses. Although you can choose to take a taxi, bus or monorail, most of the city centre can be reached on foot from the large hotels. This way it is easier to get the feel of Seattle and to begin to see why, increasingly, people are finding it so desirable a place in which to live.

Downtown Seattle

Like any self-respecting port, Seattle is liveliest along the **waterfront**. More than 90 piers stretch some 80 km (50 miles) along the shores of Elliott Bay, which gives access out to the Pacific. A drive along the Alaskan Way follows the sweeping coast-line northwards, but the panoramic route on the Alaskan Way viaduct high above sea level pays extra dividends, with the splendours of Puget Sound and the snowcapped mountains unfolding in the distance.

Life at the depths is brought up to eye level at the **Aquarium** (Pier 59). Stop by to feast your eyes on octopus, sharks, eels, seals and salmon, or sink into the total surround of a 3-D film on the 30-m (100-ft) high screen of the **Omnidome** theatre next door —featuring a helicopter flight into the erupting crater of Mt St Helens. Pier 66, newly developed with waterfront plaza and marina, offers great views of the harbour —and of Mt Rainier, if the weather is clear.

Sooner or later, everyone comes to **Pike Place Market**, with its extravagant displays of fruit and vegetables, fish and 99

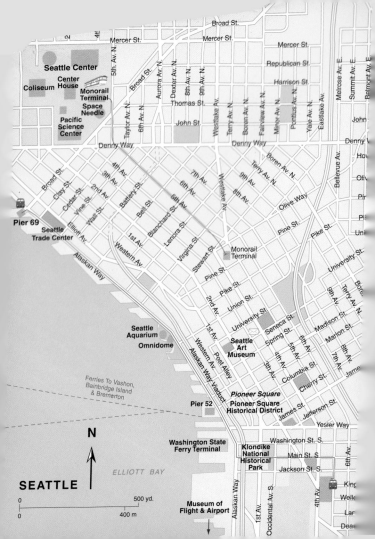

flowers. Although these stalls, which spill over on two levels, attract visitors from round the world, Pike Place is a working market which keeps locals supplied with a cornucopia of fresh foods. Small shops, like Italian delicatessens or Chinese groceries—so atmospheric they transport you thousands of miles as you go through the door—stock the essentials for a multitude of national cuisines.

The **Seattle Art Museum**, housed in spanking new quarters designed by Robert Venturi at 100 University Street, displays everything from African masks to old masters and contemporary art of the US Northwest. There is also a handsome collection of Asian art.

Go south to **Pioneer Square** (First Avenue and Yeslerway), just about the only vestige of the good old days. Its Victorian redbrick has been spared the urban developers' wrecking ball, and the pleasant tree-shaded little square is surrounded by some good restaurants (both expensive and modest), quality boutiques and excellent jazz clubs. Look out for the ornate pergola, in fact a bus shelter.

You can explore Seattle's lower levels on an **Underground Tour** (from 610 First Avenue). It leads you from Doc Maynard's Pub, through the subterranean city that was burned out in 1889 and buried under today's sidewalks, streets and buildings, which were simply erected on top. You'll see old shops and façades and eerie galleries, enlivened by the guide's amusing stories of the town's beginnings. The **Klondike Gold Rush National Historic Park** (117 South Main Street) is a museum recalling the gold-fever days (Charlie Chaplin's *The Gold Rush* is screened at weekends).

To the east is the **International District**, bounded by Fourth and Eighth avenues and Main and Lane streets. It includes Chinatown and the Japanese neighbourhood. You'll find dozens of jade and jewellery shops here, and great restaurants.

Near the airport, 20 km (12 miles) south of town, the **Museum of Flight**, is housed at the original Boeing factory. It spans the whole history of flying, from early dreams to a replica of John Glenn's space capsule, with 50 full-size aircraft.

Seattle Center and Capitol Hill

The monorail takes you to the great symbol of Seattle, the 185-m (607-ft) **Space Needle** standing on a tripod, a proud relic of the 1962 World's Fair that gave Seattle a much-needed boost after its 1950s' slump. There is a revolving restaurant and an observatory at the top from which you have a splendid view across the city to the Olympic and Cascade mountain ranges dominated by Mount Rainier.

Immediately below the Needle is the **Seattle Center**, which also grew out of the World's Fair. It groups the Opera House, Playhouse, Coliseum and several museums. The **Pacific Science Center** is a spectacular structure designed by Minoru Yamasaki to house exhibits on space exploration laser technology, the oceanography of Puget Sound—and robotic dinosaurs. The **Children's Museum** brings a neighbourhood down to a child's scale.

On Capitol Hill, the **Seattle Asian Art Museum** (Volunteer Park) features Chinese and Japanese ceramics and jade, and artworks from Korea, India, Southeast Asia and the Himalaya.

Further out towards Lake Washington, the **Arboretum** in Washington Park is a haven for travellers and gardening enthusiasts alike. Even the most ardent horticulturist may not be able to identify everyone of the 5,000 species of trees and plants brought here from all around the world, but no one can fail to appreciate their beauty. At the south end of the Washington Park, the **Japanese Gardens** are a study in contemplative serenity.

Excursions

Any visit to the waterfront should include a boat ride. From the ferry terminal on Pier 52 you can take a 35-minute trip to **Bainbridge Island**, for a walk around the quaint town that has taken the name of the island (it was formerly called Winslow). From Pier 56, **harbour tours** offer a new perspective on Seattle's skyline and its incomparable setting among the natural wonders of the Olympic Peninsula and the Cascade Range. From the same pier, tours leave for **Tillicum Village**, a Northwest Coast Indian Cultural Center and restaurant on Blake Island State Marine Park, where you can partake in a traditional salmon bake. The high-tech, high-speed catamaran Victoria Clippers make the run from Pier 69 to **Victoria**, B.C. in just $2^{1}/2$ hours. (Alternatively, amphibian air service takes $1^{1}/4$ hours or less.)

Between Seattle and Vancouver, the 172 gorgeous **San Juan Islands** are scattered across the Puget Sound. Washington State Ferries link the islands to Anacortes, north of Seattle. Whale-watching cruises are available from Friday Harbour on the main island, San Juan.

An expedition to the authentically restored town of **Sultan**, 63 km (39 miles) east of the city, will take you back to gold rush days. If you prefer something more contemporary, the **winery** at Chateau Sainte-Michelle, 24 km (15 miles) northeast of Seattle, offers tours through its ultra-modern wine-making facility, as well as a chance to sample wine made from grapes grown in the Yakima Valley.

To explore the untamed wilds of the American Northwest, you have only to decide which way to turn. **Mount St Helens** lies only 265 km (165 miles) from Seattle. You can survey the countryside, devastated by the volcano's formidable eruption in May 1980, from one of two "interpretative centers" within the Gifford Pinchot National Park, as well as studying the volcano in safety, with the help of videos and photographs.

If the silhouette of Mount Rainier has proved too inviting to resist, take an excursion out to the **Mount Rainier National Park**, two hours south of town, for some exhilarating hiking on its rugged slopes. Here, too, the mountains are volcanic, but so far inactive. Further down the slopes, subalpine forests are ablaze from late spring with an amazing profusion of delicate wild flowers.

To the northeast is the equally staggering **North Cascades National Park**, with glaciers, forest and lakes and the town of Winthrop, which has reinvented its past, restoring its wooden buildings to bring you back to the Frontier era, still vivid in the exhibits of the Shafer Museum, a loghouse known locally as "the castle".

If you think you've run out of superlatives, a trip to the **Olympic Peninsula**, its National Forest and National Park are in order— 364,000 ha (900,000 acres) of rainforest and wilderness to be sampled on short walks from the car, on hikes into the interior, by canoe or on horseback. The peninsula shelters Seattle from the open sea.

Shopping

The only difficulty of shopping in Seattle is one of choice—department store, exquisite boutique or waterfront stall. Many stores sell china, sculpture and pottery, paintings and artefacts.

Indian and Inuit art, both traditional and modern, is sold in galleries, on waterfront piers and in specialist shops in Pioneer Square. Not surprisingly, the city is also famous for its sports clothing and equipment for mountaineering, fishing and hunting.

Eating Out

Seattle's restaurants reflect the city's cosmopolitan image. Naturally, seafood holds pride of place —what could surpass freshly boiled Dungeness crab from a

103

waterfront fish bar? Every chef has a speciality of the day featuring oysters, clams or Pacific salmon. European cuisines are well represented, especially French, but a meal in one of the many fine Chinese, Japanese or Polynesian restaurants can truly transport you to unimagined shores.

Coffee houses serve many kinds of coffee and often desserts and snacks as well.

Practical Information

Banks. Opening hours are from 9 a.m. to 3 p.m., Monday to Friday, but foreign traveller's cheques and currency can usually only be cashed at major branches of banks or international airports. Make sure to carry dollars or dollar traveller's cheques.

Telephone. Seattle (area code 206) is part of the US network. To call the UK, dial 011 44, then the area code (minus the initial zero) and the local number.

General editor: Barbara Ender-Jones
Layout: Luc Malherbe
Photos: covers, pp. 4, 13, 16, 25, 32, 46, 49, 52, 56,
61, 64, 67, 86, 91 Hémisphères/Gardel;
pp. 10, 18, 34, 41, 43, 68, 72, 76, 80, 97 Bernard Joliat;
p. 74 Calgary C & VB/Mike Redwood
Cartography: JPM Publications; Elsner & Schichor